Deliver Us From Evil

A Thriller

J.D. Robins

A SAMUEL FRENCH ACTING EDITION

SAMUEL
FRENCH
FOUNDED 1830

SAMUELFRENCH-LONDON.CO.UK
SAMUELFRENCH.COM

FOR AMATEUR PRODUCTION ENQUIRIES

UNITED KINGDOM AND WORLD
EXCLUDING NORTH AMERICA
plays@SamuelFrench-London.co.uk
020 7255 4302/01

Each title is subject to availability from Samuel French,

depending upon country of performance.

CHARACTERS

Diana Seaton, early 40s
Jessy Beer, indeterminate age
Ben Seaton, early 40s
Emmeline Rawlins, elderly
Meg Bestwood, early 40s
Tim Bestwood, early 40s
Peter Hamlyn, early 40s

SYNOPSIS OF SCENES

The action of the play takes place in the sitting-room of the
new rectory in the village of Wychcombe Magna

ACT I

ACT II

ACT I
Scene 1

The sitting-room of the new rectory in the village of Wychcombe Magna. A Sunday morning in late September, 8.45 a.m.

There is a door UC which leads to the hall and the rest of the house and a door DL leading to the kitchen; french windows R lead into the garden. The room is modern but the furniture traditional. There is a fireplace to one side with a coal scuttle and shovel next to it. The room is furnished with a sofa; armchairs; a desk with a lamp and papers — including a sermon and a list of builder's snags — a notepad, pens and a phone on it and a wastepaper basket beside it; a chair with a curtain draped over it and a sewing kit nearby; a coffee table and another table behind the sofa with a decanter of sherry, an unopened bottle of sherry and several glasses on it

When the Curtain *rises the room is dimly lit because the curtains are still drawn over the french windows. We hear the mournful sound of a bell tolling from the nearby church*

Diana Seaton enters from the kitchen. She is in her early forties and wearing her dressing-gown. She heads towards the door but stops and listens intently to the bell with a puzzled expression on her face. She goes towards the window. The bell stops tolling. She halts her step

Diana exits to the hall

We hear the sound of a heavy Sunday paper being pulled out of the letterbox

Diana enters from the hall with the newspaper, heading for the kitchen. She tosses the paper on to the sofa as she passes and exits into the kitchen

Diana (*off*) Felix, puss, puss puss. Oh there you are. Come in then, no? Don't you want some brekky? Have you been eating mouse? You have, haven't you? Otherwise you'd be hungry. All right, later then.

Diana enters from the kitchen. She goes to the window, and pulls back the curtains. She screams and jumps back, clutching her throat

Jessy Beer is standing outside. She is an odd-looking woman of indeterminate age wearing shapeless clothes, Wellington boots and a woollen bobble hat pulled down low on her head. She is carrying a garden rake

Go away! Can you hear me? Please go away!

Jessy cups her ear

My husband isn't here.

Jessy mimes for her to open the door

(*Shaking her head and waving Jessy away*) If you want to speak to him you must come back later.

Jessy shrugs, waves the rake and wanders off

Diana takes a moment to pull herself together, looks timidly out of the window to make sure that Jessy has gone and then exits to the kitchen

After a moment or two Jessy returns to the window. She shades her eyes and peers through the glass. She rattles the handle and then tries the door and finds, to her surprise, that it isn't locked. She opens the door a little way, steps inside and looks around the room. She goes to the desk and scans the papers lying there

Diana enters from the kitchen carrying a mug of tea. She sees Jessy and jumps, spilling the tea down her dressing-gown

Jessy! What on earth are you doing in here? You can't just wander in here like this. Get out! Now!

Jessy (*insolently*) Don' 'ee take on so, missis. You'll likely do yerself a mischief.

Diana Please don't call me missis. I'm Mrs Seaton.

Jessy (*mimicking Diana's voice*) Mrs Seaton, is it? Suit yourself. And I'm Miss Beer, to you.

Diana (*controlling herself; with dignity*) I apologize, Miss Beer. Would you leave now, please. If you need to see the rector, come back later. Or perhaps you would like me to give him a message?

Jessy I don't want to leave no messages with you, missis. I'll tell him what I got to tell him.

Diana As you wish.

Jessy makes for the window

Jessy, Miss Beer — do you know who was ringing the church bell?
Jessy Don't know. 'Tweren't me, that's for sure. I'll be back later.
Diana But do they usually have bell practice on a Sunday morning?
Jessy Ah, you never lived round 'ere, 'ave you, missis? (*She comes close to
Diana*)

Diana backs away

So you doesn't know what goes on, eh?

Jessy exits through the french windows

*Diana makes sure she has gone and closes the window. She takes several
deep breaths, then scrabbles in her dressing-gown pocket, pulls out a sheet
of foil-wrapped pills, pops two into her mouth and washes them down with
a gulp of tea. She checks the window again and picks up some mud which
Jessy has brought in on her boots and puts it in the wastepaper basket. She
sits on the sofa and pulls the Sunday paper towards her. She sips her tea*

The phone rings

Diana gets up, goes over to the desk and picks up the receiver

Diana (*into the phone*) The Rectory; Diana Seaton speaking. ... Oh, good-
morning, Mrs Bestwood. ... No, he's taking early communion over at
Fallowfield. Can I give him a message or would you like him to ring you
back? He shouldn't be long. ... Oh, that's good, I'll tell him. ... What's
that? ... The bell? Yes, I just heard it. ... I've no idea ... Practice, perhaps?
... That's right, this morning, after church. ... We shall look forward to it.

We hear the front door open

Oh, that's him now. ... No? ... Till later then, good-bye.

*Ben Seaton enters. He is the rector of Wychcombe Magna and wears a
black shirt with a clerical collar under a bright woollen sweater*

Ben Hallo, darling. I hoped you would be having a lie-in. I was going to
surprise you with a cup of tea.
Diana I've been down for a while.

Ben (*looking at her*) Everything all right?

Diana (*unconvincingly*) Of course. Oh, that was Mrs Bestwood on the phone. She says her husband got your note and will be pleased to read the lesson this morning, and they'd love to come round after church.

Ben Good, fine. I'd forgotten we'd asked them, actually.

Diana Breakfast now?

Ben No, later perhaps, just a cup of — what's that? Tea? I want to go through my sermon.

Diana I thought you'd finished it. You were up late enough.

Ben After you'd gone up, I thought I'd run through it just once more. I must have dozed off; when I woke it was gone one!

Diana laughs and exits into the kitchen

If it had that effect on me, Lord knows what it'll do to the congregation. I thought I might put in a couple of jokes, you know, liven it up a bit.

Diana (*off*) Really, Ben. Must you?

Ben Why not? They haven't heard any of my jokes yet.

Diana enters with a mug of tea

Diana Which jokes, exactly?

Ben Oh, the old ones are always the best.

Diana What? "It's goodbye from me, and goodbye from Him?" (*She points upwards*)

Ben That one always gets a laugh.

Diana looks unconvinced

(*Reading her expression*) No? Well, perhaps you're right, I can always try them out when they get to know me better.

Diana gives him the tea and glances towards the window. He notices her glance, and slowly sips the tea she's given him

Diana Ben, Mrs Bestwood also asked about the bell.

Ben Bell? What bell?

Diana The church bell. It was tolling, just before you came in. A slow toll.

Ben I wonder who that could have been? Odd — I thought Tuesday was bell practice?

Diana Yes. I thought … It was so mournful. Mrs Bestwood said it was like a death knell; she wanted to know if someone had died.

Ben Not that I know of. I'm sure I'd have heard.

Diana looks troubled

(*Looking at her keenly*) It didn't upset you. Did it?
Diana (*sharply*) Of course not. I told you, I'm all right, don't fuss.

Diana picks up the curtain from the chair, and starts to work on the hem

Ben Good. Lovely morning. If this keeps up we can take the Bestwoods out on to the terrace later.
Diana No! There are wet leaves all over the place.
Ben No problem. I'll ask Jessy to rake them up.
Diana She's been here.
Ben Jessy has?
Diana She was here a little while ago. I told her you weren't here. Ben, do we have to keep her on?
Ben I rather think we do, darling, she seems to go with the job. Apparently she worked for my predecessor for years.
Diana I know that, but — she gives me the creeps. She makes me — uncomfortable.
Ben Uncomfortable? (*He laughs*) She is a bit weird, I must say, but quite harmless, I'm sure. You have to admit it's handy for me to have someone who knows the church and the graveyard so well. She's going to turn out to be a real treasure. (*He opens the french windows and steps outside*) Yes, it's going to be warm later on, shouldn't take a tick to clear up these leaves.
Diana Ben — come in, please, close the window.
Ben What's the matter?
Diana Nothing. Honestly, nothing. It's draughty, that's all.

Ben comes in, closes the french windows and makes to lock them behind him

Diana (*shouting quickly*) Don't lock it!
Ben What?
Diana If you lock it, we'll never get it unlocked again. Remember last time.
Ben Oh, sorry, I forgot. We must get it seen to.
Diana As soon as possible. Will you ring the builder? I've started a list for him, it's on the desk. Ring him now, Ben, please.

Ben finds the list on the desk

Ben (*reading*) Things that need fixing. Window lock, hot tap ... good. I can't very well ring him on a Sunday, can I?
Diana I suppose not. Tell me about the Bestwoods.
Ben He's one of the church wardens. You've met him.

Diana Have I?

Ben When we came for the interview together. Don't you remember?

Diana Honestly, the whole thing went by in a bit of a blur; I met so many people that day. I expect I'll know him when I see him.

Ben She seems a pleasant woman. I had a few words with her after morning service last Sunday. She sent you her regards.

Diana You mean she noticed my absence.

Ben No. It wasn't like that, darling. I explained that you were still unpacking and she sympathized. Said she was still unpacking herself.

Diana That'll take her years; the old rectory seems to be crawling with workmen at the moment. I wonder why they bought it?

Ben Rather them than me, if it's anything like the old wreck we usually get with this job: leaking roof, creaking floorboards, Arctic draughts. They're welcome. Give me our brand new rectory, every time, eh, darling?

Diana Yes, yes, I'll say, a great improvement.

Ben I have a feeling that it's just what we need. A new parish, and a house with no past. A new beginning, eh?

Diana You mean, no memories. (*Pause*) No tradition either, of course.

Ben We'll make our own, you'll see. (*Changing the subject; indicating the curtain she is working on*) What are you doing?

Diana I thought these would do for the little bedroom. They just need taking up a couple of inches. You were saying about the Bestwoods?

Ben Oh, yes. He's a barrister, did I tell you? He should read the lesson well. Perhaps he'd like to do the sermon as well?

Diana Ah-huh! I'd forgotten. Well?

Ben Well what?

Diana You know perfectly well what. Early service. How many?

Ben Not bad, a few.

Diana Exactly?

Ben Seven, actually.

Diana Aha! I win!

Ben One of them took up half of a four-seater pew, couldn't we count her as two?

Diana No. That's cheating. You said nine and I said six, so I'm the nearest.

Ben OK. Twenty pence, wasn't it?

Diana No. Fifty.

Ben gives Diana fifty pence

Now, how many for Morning Service?

Ben Ah, that takes some considering. It was raining when I left for Fallowfield, first thing, but it's cleared up now, going to be lovely.

Diana So?

Ben So, I must revise my earlier estimate.

Diana You must?

Ben Definitely. If it were raining, the village people might stay away, because they usually walk to church. Whereas the people who live further off might attend. Too wet for golf or cutting the grass, and they'd have to get the car out anyway.

Diana You make it sound like a general election.

Ben There are similarities. Now, we mustn't forget to factor in our novelty value.

Diana Our novelty value?

Ben Oh, yes, that should stand us in good stead, for a while. Once they've seen all your Sunday outfits ——

Diana That won't take long!

Ben —— and got bored with my sermons ——

Ben $\Big\}$ *(together)* —— that won't take long either! ——
Diana

Ben —— we shall have lost all our box office appeal. Then it'll be down to the regulars. Bless them, and thank God for them! Still, let's make hay while the sun shines — I'll say fifty-six.

Diana Fifty-six! … Forty-three.

Ben Thanks for the vote of confidence.

Diana Rubbish. I'm just fixing it so you'll win.

The doorbell rings and Diana jumps at the noise

Ben I wonder who that is?

Diana Heaven knows, but they'd better not catch me like this. Give me your mug. I'll go through the kitchen. Give me a chance to get across the hall and don't open the door till I'm up the stairs.

Diana hurries out into the kitchen with the mugs. Ben exits into the hall

There is a pause

Diana *(off, in a fierce whisper)* Ready!

We hear a murmur of voices, off, as Ben opens the front door

Ben enters, ushering in Emmeline Rawlins, a forceful elderly woman

Ben I'm afraid my study's still piled high with boxes. Perhaps you'd like to come in here Mrs ——

Emmeline Miss.

Ben I'm sorry. Miss, er ——

Emmeline Rawlins. Emmeline Rawlins. Mother named me after Mrs Pankhurst.

Ben Really? Your mother was a suffragette?

Emmeline My grandmother was. No, Mother said she liked the name, just to annoy my father.

Ben Well, Miss — er — Rawlins, you must forgive me. It will take me a little while to get to know all my parishioners.

Emmeline I'm not a parishioner. That is, I'm not a member of your congregation.

Ben I see.

Emmeline I doubt it. I'm an atheist.

Ben After Mrs Pankhurst?

Emmeline No. After Mother. (*She looks around the room*)

Ben Well, Miss Rawlins — wait a minute — Rawlins ——

Emmeline Ah, you've already been told about the Bad Baronet, I see, I thought it wouldn't be long.

Ben No. I was thinking of all the Rawlins family tombs and memorials I've noticed in the church.

Emmeline Oh yes, that's my lot. Great churchgoers they were in those days. They ran the village and that included the church.

Ben And the Bad Baronet; he sounds intriguing, was he one of them?

Emmeline No, rather more recent. I regret to say. He's my nephew, Frank.

Ben Why the Bad Baronet?

Emmeline Sadly, he's the skeleton in the family cupboard.

Ben Why, what did he do?

Emmeline He took part in a bullion raid, some years ago. I expect you read about it, it was in all the papers. *The Sun* dubbed him "Sir Francis Rawlins, the Bad Baronet", and it's stuck.

Ben What happened to him?

Emmeline He's serving twenty years, for armed robbery.

Ben I'm sorry.

Emmeline Yes. What a wasted life, eh? He's a bit of a local celebrity. Wychcombe's only claim to fame. (*Taking stock of the room*) Well, this is an improvement, I must say. I've been dying to see it, now that it's finished.

Ben I'm sure my wife would be delighted to show you around. In fact everyone seems interested. Perhaps we should do conducted tours.

Emmeline Raise more money than a cheese and wine, I shouldn't wonder. Yes, very nice. Snug, after that great barn of a place. Don't know how Godfrey put up with those draughts.

Ben Godfrey? Of course, my predecessor, the late Reverend Godfrey Wheeler. You knew him well?

Emmeline My cousin. Previously, the living was always held by a member of the family, of course. Every Tuesday evening, for — oh, more years than

I care to remember — Godfrey and I had a regular date. I went up to the rectory and we played.

Ben Played?

Emmeline He was a most gifted violinist. Wasted on the church.

Ben (*amused*) You must miss your musical evenings.

Emmeline I do. I miss Godfrey too. He was a dear man. Nutty as a fruit cake, of course. But what a musician. There's just me now.

Ben Just you?

Emmeline I'm the last Rawlins left in the village

Ben You'll know the Bestwoods who have bought the old rectory?

Emmeline Of course. Next-door neighbours of mine, until they moved. You've met them, I daresay?

Ben Briefly, as yet.

Emmeline She's all right. You'll loathe him, of course, everybody does.

Ben Miss Rawlins, I think perhaps ——

Emmeline Meg Parkhouse, Mrs Bestwood, is a local girl. I've known her since she was a child. Her people have farmed here since God knows when. Her brother still does, come to that. Tim Bestwood's an incomer. She was a lovely girl, you know, could have had her pick. At one time I did think that Frank was ... But there, Timothy Bestwood came along and that was it. Mind you, everyone agreed he was a "good catch", as we used to say.

Ben I see ... Miss Rawlins, what can I do ——?

Emmeline Yes, naturally, you're wondering why I'm here. I live over there. (*She gestures vaguely through the window*) My cottage backs on to the churchyard. This morning I found a head in my garden.

Ben A what?

Emmeline A head. Marble. Probably an angel. Someone must have thrown it over the wall from the churchyard. I thought you ought to know.

Ben Vandals? I hadn't realized. I thought in a village like this ——

Emmeline Local yobs, I shouldn't wonder. They usually stick to graffiti in the bus shelter. I daresay they're seeing how far they can go with the new rector. You keep the church locked, of course?

Ben Well, no.

Emmeline You should. Godfrey always did.

Ben I believe that a church should be open at all times.

Emmeline Your business entirely, Mr Seaton. I told you, I don't have much use for churches, but I don't like to see the dear old relics ill-treated.

Ben Good. It's nice to know we can agree on something.

Emmeline So you'll come and collect the head this morning?

Ben Certainly.

Diana enters, dressed

Diana Oh, I'm sorry, I thought you had finished.

Ben Come in, darling. This is Miss Rawlins, a near neighbour of ours. Miss
Rawlins, my wife, Diana.

Emmeline How do you do, Mrs Seaton. I've seen you from a distance, I
thought you were younger.

Diana I'm sorry, what ——?

Emmeline Can't be helped. You look right, that's half the battle. Don't
worry, under the lights everyone drops five years, ten if we're lucky.

Diana Lights?

Emmeline Stage lights. I produce for the local group. It's an uphill struggle,
we're desperately short of talent.

Diana I really don't think I'd be much use to you ——

Emmeline Beggars can't be choosers, my dear. You should see the others.
Anyway, come along for the read-through, at least.

Ben Darling, Miss Rawlins is dying to see over the house.

Emmeline Oh, not now, my dear. Sunday is your busy day, I know that.
Some other time I'd love to give my nose a treat.

Diana Are you free later this morning, Miss Rawlins? We're having some
people in, after church, would you care to join us?

Emmeline How kind, I should love to; till later, then.

Ben I'll show you out.

Ben shows Emmeline out to the hall, making faces at Diana as he goes

Diana exits to the kitchen

Diana (*off*) Felix, Felix, puss puss puss, come in. Come on, try. There's a
good boy. Rabbit for breakfast — you like that.

*Ben enters and goes to the desk and starts to read through his sermon
again. Diana enters*

Ben Felix in?

Diana Yes, he wouldn't come in earlier. He's still a bit wary of the cat flap.
In any case, I don't think he's very hungry; he's been hunting. What were
all the faces about, by the way?

Ben Now you've done it!

Diana What have I done?

Ben Inviting Miss Rawlins here later.

Diana Oh, she's all right. I rather took to her. I might even help with her play.
Not act of course, but I could prompt. I'd get to know people.

Ben Good idea. They can't all be atheists.

Diana (*laughing*) What? Oh! How was I to know?

Ben That doesn't matter. But she gave me the distinct impression that she
didn't get on with the Bestwoods.

Diana Oh no!

Ben Don't worry. Remember, "Blessed are the peace makers". It can be the first act of my ministry in Wychcombe, to bring about a reconciliation. Now, did you say something about breakfast?

Diana Yes. Boiled egg OK?

Ben Lovely.

Diana exits to the kitchen

Jessy appears at the window carrying a placard with a crude swastika drawn on it. She waves to attract Ben's attention. He sees her and opens the french windows

Ben Come in, Jessy, looking for me?

Jessy S'right.

Ben What can I do for you?

Jessy Them 'ooligans.

Ben Hooligans?

Jessy Bin in the churchyard, messing wiv a grave.

Ben Yes, I've heard. Is there much damage?

Jessy 'Er 'ead's gone.

Ben It was thrown over the hedge into Miss Rawlins's garden. She just came round to tell me.

Jessy Ar, saw 'er leavin'. Found this, an'all.

Jessy hands Ben the placard

Ben A swastika? Where did you find this.

Jessy On the angel; 'ung round her neck, t'was.

Ben How juvenile. Jessy, do you know who was tolling the bell, earlier?

Jessy 'Tweren't me. An' I told 'er so. I 'eard 'un though. You best lock the church.

Ben That's the second time I've been told that this morning. Decapitating angels, planting swastikas and tolling death knells may be in poor taste, but it's a far cry from desecrating a church.

Jessy T'old rector 'ad 'un locked.

Ben So I'm told. But I'm the *new* rector.

Jessy Suit yerself.

Diana enters and recoils with alarm when she sees Jessy

Diana I didn't know you were here. I didn't hear the doorbell.

Jessy I never rung.

Ben It's all right, Diana, I let Jessy in through the window.

Diana It's not all right. We have two doors. One at the front and one at the back. In future, kindly ring at either one of them.

Ben Diana, my dear ——

Diana I don't want garden dirt trodden into the floor. Please do as I say.

Jessy Aw'right missis. I'll go round Miss Rawlins, fetch back the 'ead. I'll take t' old barrow.

Diana What head?

Ben We had some damage in the churchyard last night, dear. The head was knocked off a marble angel.

Diana How disgusting!

Ben Is there any family who ought to be told, Jessy?

Jessy No. I reckon that lot all moved away. (*She turns towards the window*)

Ben Perhaps you'd better use the back door, Jessy.

Jessy Aw'right.

Jessy exits into the kitchen

Ben Weren't you a little hard on her, dear?

Diana No. (*She shivers*) I told you. She gives me the creeps. She's always snooping around.

Ben Snooping? Really, darling ——

Diana You aren't here all the time, but she is. She peers through the window when I'm here alone, and this morning I found her here, in the room. She's spying on us.

Ben Diana, you're imagining it. She's rather strange, I'll admit, but she means well.

Jessy suddenly appears from the kitchen carrying several heads of garlic

Jessy I let yer cat out. Aw'right?

Diana jumps

Ben Thank you, Jessy.

Diana No. It isn't all right. We're trying to train him to use the cat flap.

Jessy Well, he don't like that contraption, thass plain enough. An' I picked up they onions, missis.

Diana Onions?

Jessy Dropped 'em, aw' round the back door, you 'ad.

Jessy puts the garlic on the coffee table and exits into the kitchen

Diana There you are! Any excuse to pry. And I don't know what she's talking about. I haven't dropped any onions. (*She sees the swastika placard*) Ben, what's this?

Ben Jessy found it, in the churchyard, some silly joke I expect ——

The phone rings and Ben answers it. During the conversation, Diana picks up the garlic and the placard and examines them. She stares at them, mesmerized

(*Into the phone*) Rectory, Ben Seaton here. ...Oh, hallo again, Miss Rawlins. ...I've just sent Jessy over to collect it, she's taking the wheelbarrow and should be with you any minute. ... What? ... Well, I didn't think you'd mind. ... She'd already seen the damage. ... What a pleasant surprise. ... No, of course we don't mind, bring him along. ... Delighted to meet him. ... See you both later. Goodbye. (*He puts the phone down. To Diana*) Miss Rawlins. She doesn't seem to relish a visit from Jessy any more than you do. Poor Jessy, she must be using the wrong deodorant. Miss Rawlins actually rang to ask if she could bring her nephew along later. He's turned up unexpectedly, or something. You don't mind, do you, darling?

Diana is still staring, mesmerized, at the garlic

Di?
Diana These aren't onions.
Ben What aren't?
Diana These. Jessy said she found them round the back door. But they aren't onions.
Ben What are they, then?
Diana Garlic.
Ben Super, what's for lunch, something exotic?
Diana You don't understand — I didn't drop them.
Ben Well, somebody else must have, what of it?
Diana Why? Why garlic?
Ben (*lightly*) Perhaps they think we're vampires.
Diana Don't, Ben! Don't joke. It isn't funny.
Ben Sorry, darling, but really ——
Diana First a grave is disturbed, and now this. (*She waves the garlic and the placard at Ben*)
Ben What? Oh, really, Diana, there is no connection.
Diana There is, there must be. Ben, I'm frightened, someone has done this deliberately.
Ben It's just some silly ——
Diana It's not, I know it. Someone is trying to scare us and ——
Ben For heaven's sake, Di. Stop being so fanciful. It's just some village lads who've been watching the wrong sort of videos. You know I'm right. Now, what about my breakfast, eh?

We can see that Diana is not convinced by Ben's reassurances

Diana exits into the kitchen

Ben picks up the garlic and the placard and carries them over to the desk. He examines them thoughtfully

CURTAIN

SCENE 2

The same. After Morning Service on the same day. 12.15 pm

The CURTAIN *rises. The curtain Diana has been altering has been removed*

Diana enters followed by Meg Bestwood. They have come straight from church. Meg is a handsome woman with a down-to-earth, jolly manner. She carries a bag

Meg Oh! What a charming room, so light and airy.
Diana Yes. It faces south. It's such a lovely day, Ben thought we could take our drinks out on to the terrace. Not much of a garden yet, of course, but the piece immediately outside the window has been paved for us.
Meg Well at least it's tidy. We haven't even begun to clear the jungle at the old rectory. By the way, is that your cat I've seen stalking through the undergrowth?
Diana A large shaggy ginger creature?

Meg nods

That'll be Felix.
Meg Felix? I thought Felix was black and white.
Diana Yes, he was, but our Felix was named by someone — who didn't know that. (*She looks away to the garden*)

Pause. Meg waits for Diana to go on

I — er — I hope he hasn't done any damage?
Meg What? Oh, impossible. That garden hasn't been touched for years. The Reverend Wheeler said he liked it wild, to attract the birds. Potty about them he was. He once accosted old Mrs Clegg and told her to keep her tomcat from chasing his birds.
Diana And did she?

Meg She looked at him over her specs and said, "'Tis 'is nature, Rector. If you don't like it, complain to your boss. He made my Tom, same as he made them birds."

They both laugh

Always ready with a pithy remark was Mrs Clegg. I remember one winter, a gale brought down the weather vane on top of the church tower. After some months it was replaced. We were all standing round, after church, admiring it, all freshly gilded, and glinting in the sunshine. Up strolls Mrs Clegg and remarks to one and all "See Rector's got his old cock up again."
Diana She sounds priceless; I must meet her.
Meg Sadly, you're too late; she died last year. But we still have a few local characters — oh, that reminds me, I've got something for you. (*She fishes in her bag and pulls out a small flat package wrapped in gift paper*)
Diana For me? How sweet of you.
Meg Nothing much, just a welcome to Wychcombe Magna.

Diana unwraps the package; it contains a small flat plaque. Diana holds it, looking at it dubiously

Diana What is it?
Meg It's the Wychcombe Familiar.
Diana Familiar?
Meg You'll soon become familiar with it, at any rate. It's depicted several times around the church. It's the gargoyle to the left of the porch, and inside, there are two carved into the ceiling bosses, and there's another on one of the pew ends. Godfrey Wheeler had a batch like this made and we used to sell them to raise money for the church appeal. Almost everyone in Wychcombe has one. You tack it to the front door, or the back one, it doesn't matter which. Supposed to bring good luck, or ward off evil spirits, depending on your point of view.
Diana (*obviously mildly disturbed by the Familiar*) Well, thank you.

Ben enters with Tim Bestwood. Tim is confident and successful

Tim Rattling good sermon, Padre. Specially liked the jokes.

Ben gives Diana a smug glance

The choir was in good form too, I thought. Old Josh certainly licks them into shape.
Ben Josh? Oh, that would be Mr Larkin. The local plumber, right?

Tim Plumber and choirmaster. Funny thing is, he can't sing a note himself. Bad case of strangulated canticles. Good man to keep in with though, worth his weight in tap washers. Well, I must say (*looking around the room*) the church commissioners have done you proud. Splendid job. Makes damned good business sense too: sell off their derelict property — always enough idiots like my wife, willing to pay inflated prices — then invest the money in well-built modern stuff. Didn't even have to buy the land. Just lopped off a hunk of the old rectory garden. I mean, who's got time for gardens that size any more? They'd have done it years ago, but Godfrey had private money so he kept the rectory going, after a fashion.

Diana But the old house will be beautiful when the work is finished.

Tim I've no doubt you're right, Mrs Seaton. I should live to enjoy it.

Ben Surely it won't take that long?

Tim You mistake me. At the moment, we have no roof, so if we have any serious rain, I'm liable to drown. Then she'll have the windows out and we'll spend Christmas in a howling gale. Should I survive that ordeal, all the floors will be ripped up in the New Year. A broken leg will be the least I can expect.

Ben You sound as if you speak from experience.

Tim Oh, bitter experience, bitter, I assure you. This is the fourth old wreck she'll have converted since we were married.

Ben (*to Meg and Tim*) Can I offer you a sherry? Or would you prefer coffee?

Meg Sherry would be lovely, thanks.

Tim Sherry!

Meg kicks him hard

Ah, sherry, splendid.

Ben pours out four glasses of sherry and hands them round during the following

Meg It's a hobby of mine, restoring old houses.

Tim Hobby! It's her life's work, but this one is by far her *magnum opus*.

Meg Well it keeps me busy. Tim's away half the week and with the children away from home now, I have time on my hands. Do you have any children?

Diana (*quickly*) No.

Tim Very wise. I could have been a rich man if I'd never let Meg persuade me that we needed a family. Restoring old houses? Small change, compared with the brats. (*Obviously very proud of his children*) With our kids, it's "Hallo give me and goodbye send me!"

Ben (*hastily*) Miss Rawlins mentioned that you used to live in a house next to her. Did you restore that one too?

Tim So, you've met Lady Bountiful, have you? Yes, she lived next door. Nice little cottage, but quite a comedown, after the loony bin up on the hill.

Meg My husband has such an elegant turn of phrase. Wychcombe Hall used to be the Rawlins family home, and then it was used as a mental hospital for a while, but now it's a special school.

Diana Of course, the Hartford Institute — I didn't realize …

Meg You know it?

Diana Yes, well I had an interview there on Friday.

Tim Interview?

Ben Diana is a speech therapist.

Tim Are you going to work up at the Hall?

Diana Just three days a week, after Christmas. What a beautiful house, that wonderful entrance with the staircase.

Meg You should have seen it in the old days.

Tim Meg's got a soft spot for the Hall, and the family. Haven't you, dear? Used to be invited up to the Hall for Christmas parties, with the tenants' children, eh?

Meg Yes. It was like fairyland, there was a huge tree in the hall, hanging with lights and presents. Old Sir Daniel and Lady Rawlins, Em's parents, used to hand out ——

Tim Poor old Em's been living among the peasantry ever since I've known her. But Meg, and the older locals, still tug their forelocks. Em carries on with her good works, *noblesse oblige*, you know.

Meg As you will have gathered, Tim is paranoid on the subject of Miss Rawlins. When we lived next door, he kept up a pointless running battle over the boundary fence.

Tim It was not pointless. That's the trouble with these feudal types. The law applies to everyone but them. Old witch!

Diana Witch?

Meg Shut up, Tim. (*To Ben and Diana*) Take no notice of him. She's really quite a jolly old soul, just a bit eccentric, like a lot of these old families.

Tim Eccentric! The whole family's certifiable. Don't know which was worse, her or old Godfrey Wheeler.

Ben The rector?

Tim Yes, he was the fool of the family who went in to the church! Ha! (*Realizing that his comments are not exactly apt in present company*) Course, those were the old days.

Meg How did you meet Miss Rawlins? She never goes to church.

Tim Don't tell me, she's given up the black arts for the solace of the sacraments?

Meg Tim!

Ben No. I haven't made a convert, yet. She woke this morning to find the head of an angel lying on her lawn.

Tim A miracle?

Ben No. A vandal.

Tim Blighters! Just let me catch them. Must have been them mucking about with the bells, too.

Meg An angel? That must be the poor little Taylor girl's grave.

Diana It was a child's grave?

Meg Yes, well, an old family grave, but she was buried there. Such a tragic accident. Nice family, they moved away after it happened. I've often wondered what became of them.

Ben Yes, well I must ask you to brace yourselves; not knowing about the feud, Diana asked Miss Rawlins to join us. She should be here at any moment.

Diana And her nephew.

Meg (*startled*) Her nephew!

Tim Which nephew?

Diana How many has she got?

Tim Two.

Ben Well, not the Bad Baronet at any rate.

Tim Oh, you've heard about him, then.

Meg It must be Peter. Frank's brother.

Tim Peter's a decent enough sort, not that we see much of him. Chalk and cheese, those two. Their father, Em's brother, was killed in an air crash, along with his wife. The boys were quite young at the time. Anyway when the brother's affairs were settled, it turned out that the estate was pretty near bankrupt. The Hall and all the land had to be sold.

Meg Miss Rawlins moved to Pugsley's Cottage and took them in. She and the old rector more or less brought the boys up between them.

Tim "Brought them up" is putting it a bit strongly, from what I've heard. According to the locals, they ran wild.

Meg That's not true, Tim — you didn't know them then.

Tim Ha! You would jump to their defence. Meg here was their partner in crime.

Meg It was just high spirits ——

Tim That's right, just the young gentlemen from the Hall, up to their jolly japes, boys will be boys. High spirits! These days they'd have been slapped with an ASBO, if half of what I've heard is true.

Meg Tim! You do exaggerate. Mind you, we were little tykes, up to all sorts of mischief — well Frank was, he was always the ringleader; Peter and I used to follow.

Tim I don't know how you were allowed to get away with it.

Meg Frank's asthma used to come in handy. When things started to get tough, he'd have an attack, and by the time they'd dealt with that, whatever we'd done would have been forgotten.

Ben What happened when they grew up?

Tim Frank went into the army; Em hoped that it would steady him. It did for a while, I believe, but inevitably, he came out under a cloud. Anyway, after that, Em bailed him out of one scrape after another. Finally told him she'd paid up for the last time, and he was on his own. So, he slung his hook, and dropped right out of sight. That was years before the robbery.

Diana And Peter?

Meg Took a very different path. He was the academic one. He teaches at some American university.

Tim So when you said Em's nephew, it gave me quite a turn. If Frank has kept his nose clean, he could be out by now. I wasn't thinking of Peter.

Diana Poor Miss Rawlins.

The doorbell rings

Oh, well, here goes.

Meg Don't worry, my dear, Tim can behave, if he has to.

Diana Ben, why don't you take Meg and Tim out on the terrace, we'll join you in a minute.

Diana exits into the hall

Tim (*finishing his glass*) This is very good sherry. Surprisingly good.

Ben Glad you approve. My brother's an importer. We get a case every Christmas and birthdays — if we didn't, it would be Tesco's best! Let me top you up.

Tim By all means. Don't usually drink the stuff, when Meg said sherry, my heart sank ——

Meg Tim!

Ben tops up Tim's glass

Ben, Tim and Meg exit through the french doors on to the terrace

Diana enters with Emmeline and Peter. Peter is a pleasant-looking man of about Meg's age, with a quiet and courteous manner. He wears glasses and has the slightly myopic and stooped look associated with with a stereotypical professor of archaeology

Emmeline This is very civil of you to invite us, Mrs Seaton. This is my nephew, Peter. Peter, Mrs Seaton, our new rector's wife.

Peter Kind of you to have me.

Diana Not at all. Miss Rawlins says you have only recently returned to this country.

Emmeline Got the shock of my life. He turned up this morning right out of the blue.

Diana A lovely surprise for you. Are you here for long?

Peter Just for a day or two this time, but I hope to have a week or two later, if Aunt Em will have me.

Diana You're not on holiday then?

Peter Not exactly, I'm taking a year's sabbatical.

Emmeline Peter teaches at a university in California.

Diana Really? So what do you intend to do with your year's sabbatical?

Peter Travel around Europe; I've a series of lectures lined up.

Diana What is your subject?

Peter I'm an archaeologist.

Diana Oh, you know about old buildings? You must tell me all about the church.

Peter Twelfth century is a bit late for me. You'll have to ask Aunt Em, she and Uncle Godfrey were the experts.

Emmeline That's true — at least, Godfrey was. He wrote a most interesting history of the parish. He was always going to do something about getting it published. Silly old fool, he never got round to it. I've got a copy somewhere. I'll dig it out and let you have it. It's quite short.

Peter That's because nothing much ever happened here. The tomb in the Lady Chapel belongs to Sir Hugo de Wykham. Rumour has it that he missed the crusades because he was down with measles. There were a few fatalities during the Black Death. Supposed to be a plague pit somewhere, but nobody quite knows where. Frank and I used to dig up everyone's garden, looking for it. Oh, and a fifteenth century ancestor of ours was burnt at the stake.

Diana Really? What for?

Emmeline Witchcraft.

Diana Witchcraft!

Peter Yes, he was the parish priest and they say he took to flying round the church tower at the full moon. Eventually, some of the locals got fed up with him and petitioned the bishop against low-flying clergy.

This is obviously a well-rehearsed family joke. Diana is not amused but Emmeline and Peter don't notice

Diana (*smiling politely*) Shall we go and join the others? The Bestwoods are here.

Emmeline Marvellous! Tim Bestwood! Lead me to him! You remember him, Peter, that dreadful man who used to live next door?

They exit on to the terrace. Diana enters and exits into the kitchen

Diana (*off*) Oh, there you are. All right, Mummy's coming. Come in, then. Well, come in if you're going to. Silly old puss. All right, stay out then.

Diana enters with a plate of snacks. Ben enters from the terrace

Ben Good job you've got a birthday soon, darling.
Diana Birthday? Why?
Ben We'll get the cellar restocked. Otherwise we're never going to keep up with Tim Bestwood.
Diana How's it going between the Bestwood and Rawlins camps?
Ben No problem. They're the best of enemies. (*He picks up the sherry decanter. Indicating a new bottle on the table*) Open that, please, love. Bring it out when you come. (*He notices the Familiar that Diana has left on the desk*) What's that?
Diana Meg brought it for me. It's a "familiar", or something. You put it on the door to ward off evil spirits; some sort of local custom, she said.
Ben Ugly little brute. Don't fancy him on my door.

Ben exits to the terrace with the snacks

Diana tries to open the sherry bottle and struggles with it

Peter enters from the terrace

Peter Here, let me do that.
Diana Thank you, I always break a nail. I know, I'll fetch a knife.

Diana exits to the kitchen

Peter idly picks up Diana's list of snags from the desk and reads it

Diana enters with a small knife

Diana (*holding the knife out to Peter*) Here.
Peter Thanks. (*He takes the knife and puts the list back on the desk*)
Diana My snag list. They've promised to come back next week and put the little things right.
Peter Not too many, I hope. How do you like your new house?
Diana Very much. Of course you won't have seen it before.
Peter I had no idea they were even thinking of building a new one. I haven't managed to get over here for some time. I got the shock of my life when I looked out of Aunt Em's kitchen window and saw a new house.
Diana You must have known the old rectory well.

Peter I'll say. Frank and I knew every inch of Uncle Godfrey's garden, at one time. Although now (*looking out of the window*) I can't quite work out where we are standing in relation to the old house.

Diana The plans will show it; wait a minute, they're here somewhere.

Diana takes a set of architect's plans from the desk drawer and spreads them out on the table behind the sofa. Peter looks over her shoulder

(*Pointing*) There.

Peter Let me see. I think ... Oh, yes, that's right. (*He turns the plan around and peers out of the window and then back to the plan. Pointing*) This was the shrubbery, where we're standing — a sort of thicket. This line of trees, here, that's all that's left.

Diana That's a shame, I hate to see trees cut down.

Peter It was mostly scrub. A paradise for us, when we were children. You could get right inside and be hidden from the house. Frank and I had a den here. We called it Dingly Dell.

Ben (*off*) Di, where is that sherry?

Diana (*calling*) Coming, darling. (*To Peter*) I was a town child myself, but I can see it must have been paradise. Felix thinks it still is, after our last parish.

Peter Felix, your son?

Diana No. I have no son. Felix is our cat. Excuse me.

Diana exits to the terrace

Peter continues to examine the plans

Meg enters from the terrace

Meg Peter?

Peter turns. For a moment Meg looks puzzled

Peter Hallo, Meg. You haven't changed a bit.

Meg No, nor you ... It's nice to see you. It's been a while. You'll notice some changes since you were last here.

Peter Yes, indeed. Aunt Em says that you're now living at the old rectory. Tell me, does it still have that delicious smell?

Meg I don't know, what smell was that?

Peter I couldn't say, really. It was just the rectory. I've always associated it with the long summer holidays, exploring the attics and pinching Uncle Godfrey's cigars. We used to smoke them and drink his best port, down in Dingly Dell.

Meg I remember.

Peter Of course you do! I seem to remember that the port didn't agree with you.

Meg Yes. Well we needn't go in to that. As to the smell, I think it must have been a mixture of mildew and dry rot. And yes, it's still there.

Peter Oh, good. Can I come and have a sniff?

Meg Certainly, but you'd better come quick, the builders are just about to exorcise it.

Peter What a shame! You'll destroy the character of the old place.

Meg and Peter exit to the terrace

There comes the sound of someone knocking on the back door. Nobody hears it. Another knock

Jessy (*off*) 'Allo, anybody 'ome?

Jessy enters from the kitchen and comes tentatively into the room. She goes to the french windows but decides against disturbing anybody. She picks up a pen from beside the telephone and laboriously writes a note. She props it up against the telephone and goes towards the kitchen

Diana enters from the terrace and starts with annoyance when she sees Jessy

Diana What are you doing here?

Jessy I knocked.

Diana That doesn't mean you can just ——

Jessy Twice.

Diana That still doesn't give you the right to ——

Jessy (*coming close to Diana and seeming to menace her*) I come 'ere to bring the key to the vestry. He won't have church locked, so I locked vestry. Now you just tell 'im that, right? An don't you go telling him tales about me. I'm on to you missis. You'd better watch yerself, I'm warning you. 'ere. (*She produces a key and thrusts it at Diana*) An' I seen Alf Vench. 'E does the stone. 'E'll put 'er old 'ead on again. Alf'll be round in morning.

Diana (*whispering*) Go away, please.

Jessy Right. You tell 'un. (*She turns to go*) And don't you forget, accidents happen here in the country.

Diana Are you threatening me?

Jessy No. Why would I do that? I'm just telling you. Things 'appen. That little girl, her what her grave got damaged; bad thing 'appened to 'er 'an all.

Emmeline enters

Knocked down, she were, by a car. They didn't never find who done it. She were lying there in the road she were. Bin there an hour or more they reckoned. All covered in blood, I seed her. Died in the hambulance.

Diana Oh my God!

Jessy 'Orrible it were. I reckoned you'd want to know.

Diana Oh, dear God. (*She sways*)

Jessy You want to be careful how you go.

Diana Get out of here. Do you hear me? Get out of here, with your filthy tricks and disgusting stories. Don't you ever come here again.

Jessy (*to Emmeline*) She mazed, or something? (*She indicates "mad" by revolving her finger near her temple*)

Emmeline Mrs Seaton, are you all right?

Diana What?

Emmeline Can I get you anything? Look, you'd better sit down. I'll fetch your husband.

Diana No!

Emmeline But you're not well.

Diana Why does everyone say I'm not well? Can't you see? She's evil, she's trying to scare me. I'm sorry, excuse me. Please.

Diana exits to the hall

Emmeline follows Diana to the door, looking after her, then turns on Jessy

Emmeline What are you trying to do to that poor woman? What were you telling her when I came in?

Jessy I were telling her 'bout that Taylor girl. Didn't tell 'er who done it though. But we both know, don't we?

Emmeline What do you mean?

Jessy Oh, thass the way you want it, is it? Pretending you don't know.

Emmeline I don't know what you're talking about, of course I don't know.

Jessy Then why 'ave you been shelling out all these years then, you answer me that?

Emmeline You mean ... ? Oh, God! (*She is visibly shaken*) You're lying.

Jessy Lying, am I? Don't you forget, I saw him. Driving away he was, early in the morning.

Emmeline I didn't know, I swear I didn't know.

Jessy Well now you do, and I reckon it's going to cost you. That daft cow, she'll tell 'er 'usband and he'll likely sack me, so I'm going to need some extra, several thousands this time. Let's say five, that should see me through for a bit.

Emmeline But I haven't got that sort of money, besides ... (*She makes up her mind, and is very angry*) No. Never. You've gone too far this time,

Jessy. Tell who you like, but you've seen the last penny from me. Mrs Seaton's right, you're a disgusting, vicious creature, and I've paid you for the last time.

Peter enters and listens in amazement to the following

If you've lost your job, you've only yourself to blame and I for one am delighted. You've been asking for it for a long time. Now get out of here, do you hear me?

Jessy Right you are, but you'll be sorry, an' so will he, I'll see to that.

Jessy exits through the kitchen door

Peter What on earth was that all about?

Emmeline Nothing, Peter, don't you worry about it.

Peter But it can't be nothing.

Emmeline Just a minor dispute. (*Having had time to think*) She says I owe her for some hedge trimming she did for me — nothing, too trivial for words.

Ben enters with Meg and Tim

Ben Getting a bit cold out there. That's the trouble at this time of year. Gets a bit chilly once the sun goes in.

Meg We must be getting home, in any case. I can smell burnt roast beef from here.

Ben Must you? Diana ... (*He notices she is not there*) Did anyone see where she went?

Emmeline Upstairs, I think. She seemed a bit upset. Jessy Beer was here with her when I came in.

Ben Jessy? Jessy upset her? What did she say?

Emmeline She was telling Mrs Seaton about the death of the little Taylor girl.

Ben The little girl whose grave was damaged, you mean? How did she die, by the way?

Meg It was a hit and run accident. So sad. They never found out who was responsible.

Ben When did it happen?

Meg Ten years ago? About that, as far as I remember. Right, Tim, we're off.

Tim Right you are, m'dear. Bye, Peter, nice to see you. Oh and I look forward, sometime, to continuing our discussion about village development, Miss Rawlins ——

Emmeline I told you. The whole scheme will completely ruin Wychcombe.

Tim That's just your opinion.

Emmeline Oh, no, there are a lot of people round here who agree with me.

Tim Only because they wouldn't dare to disagree with you.

The discussion starts to become heated

Emmeline Nobody wants to see the village swamped with hideous new houses.

Tim How do you know they would be hideous? That's typical of you and your nimby friends. People need somewhere to live, local young people ——

Emmeline Oh, no! Don't give me that spurious argument. You know very well, the local young people won't be able to afford them.

Tim Well, that's a pity, because it's their parents and grandparents who are making a killing by selling off their land.

Emmeline That's beside the point. The whole lot will be sold to incomers, or worse still as weekend homes.

Tim And you wouldn't want that, I'm sure. Incomers and weekenders don't know their place, do they? Not enough forelock-tugging to suit you.

Emmeline Well don't you think you're going to sway the Parish Council ——

Meg (*interrupting firmly*) Tim! We're going.

Tim Well, I was just ——

Meg Now!

Tim Oh, very well, love. Pity, I was just getting into my stride.

Peter Really, Auntie, you seem to be in a particularly belligerent mood, something rattled your cage?

Meg They're one as bad as the other. Say goodbye to Diana for us. Tell her I'll give her a ring later this afternoon.

Ben Yes, yes, I'm sorry she … I could call ——

Meg No, don't disturb her, just say goodbye for us, and thank her, will you?

Peter Thank you so much, Mr Seaton. Hope your wife's feeling better soon.

Meg and Peter exit into the hall followed by Ben

Emmeline (*moving to leave*) Those barns have been there for hundreds of years; you come along and buy them, and in no time, they've been demolished. God knows how you got permission. It's obvious to me that something very dodgy went on in the planning office.

Tim (*incensed*) *What* the hell are you implying?

Emmeline You work it out, but planning officers aren't the best paid local government workers.

Tim My God! If that doesn't take the biscuit, all I have done is to buy some property that was for sale and apply for planning permission, and you've got the gall to accuse me of corruption!

Emmeline If the cap fits ——

Tim The words "glass houses" and "stones" come to mind. I didn't bribe
anyone, but even if I had, at least I didn't storm the planning office in the
early hours of the morning wearing a mask, swinging a gun and bashing
some poor bastard over the head. Don't forget that's what your precious
nephew did.

Emmeline Frank didn't injure anyone; he wasn't the one who used violence.

Tim Oh, you'd defend him if he'd shot the Pope. He's your Frank, your blue-
eyed boy. And that makes armed robbery OK, does it?

Meg (*off*) Tim! Shut up!

Tim and Emmeline exit into the hall

*Diana enters from the kitchen. She is weeping silently. She goes to the
window and looks out with her back to the room. We see her shoulders
shaking*

Ben enters

Diana (*turning round*) Ben.
Ben I know, darling, I heard.
Diana Oh, Ben.

Ben takes Diana in his arms and rocks her like a child

CURTAIN

SCENE 3

The same. The following Monday. Dusk

When the CURTAIN *opens, the living-room is gloomy, with the lights not yet
turned on. The curtains are drawn back. It is raining heavily. The curtain
Diana is altering is once again draped over one of the armchairs*

*A figure looking very much like Jessy enters stealthily through the french
windows, moves towards the armchair and puts a dead rat in the folds of the
curtain on the chair*

Diana (*off*) Felix, Felix, Felix.

*At the sound of Diana's voice, the figure exits rapidly through the french
windows, leaving them wide open*

Come on puss, puss, puss.

We hear the sound of a spoon being rattled on a plate

Come on, my boy, where are you? Nosh time, lovely nosh. Felix, where are you? You'll get soaked out there.

Diana enters from the kitchen, heading for the hall door. She hears the rain, turns to the french windows and gives a slight gasp when she notices that they are wide open. She closes them, then stoops down and picks up a wet leaf and some garden earth from the carpet just inside the window. She gives the carpet a rub with her hand. Straightening up, she looks with puzzlement at the leaf and the earth in her hand

Ben (*off*) Hallo, darling, I'm back.

Ben enters, switching on the room lights as he passes the switch

God, what a day. The road from Fallowfield is virtually under water; I had to come round the other way. Did you manage to get a rest, put your feet up for a bit? Good, make you feel better, after a bad night.

Diana doesn't answer; she is still examining the wet leaf in her hand

What have you got there?
Diana Ben, did you come in this way earlier and leave the window open?
Ben No, I told you, I only just got back. Why?
Diana The window was open. Good job the rain is blowing the other way, we might have had a soaked carpet. (*She heads for the kitchen*) I've just made some tea.

Diana exits into the kitchen

Ben Any sign of Felix? (*During the following he tries the window to make sure it's shut and pulls the curtains across*) Can't think where he could be, he didn't come in for last night's supper. Mind you, with all this wildlife around, I wouldn't put it past him to do a spot of self-catering. Still, in this weather ——

The phone rings

(*Answering it; into the phone*) Rectory, Ben Seaton speaking. ... Oh, good of you to ring, are you sure it's convenient? ... About ten minutes, then. ... See you, 'bye.

Diana enters with two mugs of tea which she puts on the coffee table

Diana Did you ring the builder about that window?
Ben Yes, this morning. He wasn't there so I left a message on his answerphone. He hasn't rung back?
Diana (*sharply*) If he had, I wouldn't be asking, would I?
Ben (*not retaliating; mildly*) It's too late to ring him back now, I'll try again in the morning. I'll just hang my raincoat over the boiler, I think.

Ben exits into the kitchen

Diana takes a sip of her tea and then decides that the curtain she is mending needs tidying. She picks the curtain up to fold it and the rat falls out and lands at her feet. Diana looks at the rat and shrieks

Diana Ben! Oh my God! Ben, quickly!
Ben (*rushing in*) What? What is it?
Diana Look! (*She points at the rat*)
Ben Good heavens! It's a rat.
Diana Take it away, take it away from me, it's horrible …
Ben It's only a dead rat.
Diana Get it out of here. Get that ghastly thing out of here.
Ben (*going to the fireplace and taking the shovel out of the coal scuttle*) Diana darling, you've seen a rat before, why are you getting into such a state? (*He scoops up the rat with the shovel and moves towards the kitchen*)
Diana How did it get there, tell me that? Who put it there?
Ben Nobody put it there. Felix must have brought it in. It's a present.
Diana Felix?
Ben Yes. Cats do that. He's brought in mice before, you know that.
Diana But this is a rat. Someone put it there. Someone put it there deliberately.
Ben (*reproachfully*) Oh, Di. Let me get rid of it.

Ben exits into the kitchen with the shovel

Diana sits on the sofa, shivering and warming her hands round the mug of tea

Ben enters and looks at her

Are you cold? Shall I turn the heating up?

Diana doesn't reply. Ben wanders over to the window and peeks through the curtains

It's not letting up any — still pouring. I think Sunday must have been a flash in the pan. What was it your mother used to call it? I know, an Indian summer. Don't you remember what an old witch she was with her weather forecasts?

Diana flinches. Ben realizes that he's said quite the wrong thing

If it ever stops raining, we must decide about the roses. They might look good edging the terrace, or it might be better to let the lawn come right up and plant the roses down the side. What do you think, darling?

Diana She did it.

Ben What?

Diana Jessy did it. She put the rat here.

Ben (*trying to be patient*) Now Diana, you know that's not true; why on earth would Jessy plant a dead rat in our living-room?

Diana To frighten me; she hates me.

Ben shakes his head and turns away

So you're not going to do anything?

Ben Darling, we discussed it. We were up half last night talking about it. I thought you understood. There's nothing I can do.

Diana Yes there is. You could get rid of her.

Ben Di, be sensible, what reason could I give?

Diana I can't bear having her near me. She threatens me; you don't know, you don't see it.

Ben See what?

Diana Butter wouldn't melt in her mouth when you're around, but she's fooling you, I tell you. It's all an act.

Ben Diana, I have to tell you, you're being ridiculous.

Diana You don't believe me, do you? Nobody believes me.

Ben I do, darling, really I do.

Diana No you don't. You think I'm hallucinating.

Ben I'm sure you sincerely believe what you say, darling. I believe that for some reason, you've got it in to your head that Jessy's strange manner is menacing. If only I could make you see ——

Diana That it's all in my imagination? Is that what you mean?

Ben No, not exactly. I'm just asking you consider the possibility that you might be mistaken.

Diana In the meantime you're just going to let her go on persecuting me?

Ben Look, I know it upset you, to hear how that little girl died. I can understand that, but it isn't rational to take it out on Jessy. You're letting your imagination run away from you and blaming poor Jessy for an unfortunate coincidence.

Diana A coincidence? Is that what you really think?

Ben Of course.

Diana And I tell you, she knows.

Ben Oh, Di, love, how could she?

Diana Well, ask her. Ask her if she knocked the head off that angel. Ask her
if she planted the garlic. It must have been her tolling that bell, who else
could it have been?

Ben For the last time, Diana, I'm not going to sack Jessy without one iota
of proof. And that's final.

Diana So, I was right. You'll do nothing.

Ben I haven't said that. As a matter of fact, I gave Tim Bestwood a ring first
thing this morning, before he left. He's just rung to say he'll be here in a
minute. He's a churchwarden for a start, and he must have known Jessy for
years. I'm sure his advice will be sound. Now come on, darling. Why don't
you make some fresh tea? I'm sure he can do with a cup; he's coming
straight from work.

Diana I haven't time. I've things to do.

*Diana exits. Ben puts his head in his hands for a moment then exits to the
kitchen with the dirty mugs*

The doorbell rings

Ben (*off*) Come in, in here will you?

Ben enters with Tim

Very good of you to come round; I hope it wasn't too early when I rang this
morning?

Tim Good Lord, no, I'd been up for hours. The death-watch beetles start their
morning exercises early in our household.

Ben You've got death-watch beetle?

Tim Meg assures me it's only the workmen banging about up on the roof.
But I prefer to think it's a lovelorn beetle, calling to its mate.

Ben Do sit down. Would you like some tea? There's still some in the pot;
shouldn't be too stewed.

Tim No, never touch the stuff if I can help it.

Ben Coffee then? I can manage instant. I know, how about a sherry?

Tim That's the stuff! Now you're talking! So, what's the trouble?

Ben I'm after a bit of advice.

Tim If you're thinking of going to law my advice is, don't! On the other hand,
I take that back. Someone's going to have to pay for my roof.

Ben No, nothing like that, not your professional advice. It's more on a
personal level. You must have wondered about Diana's behaviour,
yesterday.

Tim I never wonder about how women behave, old chum. One of life's impenetrable mysteries.

Ben Nevertheless, it must have struck you that Diana's reaction to the story of the little girl's death was way over the top. I feel we owe you an explanation.

Tim You don't owe us anything. Unless you want to ...

Ben As you know, when I applied to come here I had been working, part-time, as a prison chaplain and prior to that, my last parish was in the Midlands, near Stoke. We left there two years ago, after our only child, our son, David, was killed in a hit and run accident.

Tim Oh. Oh, Lord! I see.

Ben He had stayed on at school for cricket practice. He was cycling home in the dusk, and was hit by a car. There were no witnesses. Unlike the poor little Taylor girl, he was killed instantly. At least we know he didn't suffer. They never traced the driver.

Tim I don't know what to say ...

Ben Diana has never really recovered. She suffered a complete breakdown at the time. Ironic, isn't it? I'm supposed to be the person who brings what comfort I can, in times of trouble. God knows I did a pretty poor job when it came to my own family. For some months she was — well, they did their best to treat her, the medication helped. Anyway, she's been a lot better recently. It all takes time, of course. I had thought, that coming here, where nobody knew about David, would help, but yesterday brought it all back.

Tim It was bound to. God! What a cruel coincidence.

Ben Exactly. The problem is, Diana doesn't accept that it was just that, a coincidence.

Tim She doesn't? But what else?

Ben As you can imagine, she's very vulnerable, still pretty fragile. It isn't that she's imagining things, it's just that, in her mind, she has strung together several completely unrelated incidents.

Tim Such as?

Ben Well, there was the tolling of the church bell, yesterday morning. Everyone heard it, but nobody seems to know who did it, or why.

Tim Gave me quite a turn. Damned odd, sounded like a death knell.

Ben takes the swastika, the garlic and the familiar out of the drawer. He holds up the swastika

Ben This was found, hanging round the neck of the damaged angel.

Tim A swastika? Good Lord! Nazis, in Wychcombe?

Ben If you look more closely, you will see that it's not a Nazi swastika. The symbol is drawn in reverse.

Tim Well?

Ben It could be a mistake, of course, but when I saw it drawn that way, it triggered something in the back of my mind. So I looked it up. The reverse swastika is regarded by some as a good luck charm. It is also a very ancient symbol used in witchcraft. (*He opens a book on the desk and shows Tim*)

Tim So it is. My sainted aunt (*laughing nervously*) I don't know which is worse, the Third Reich or witchcraft.

Ben These were found strewn around outside our back door. (*He shows Tim the garlic*)

Tim What are they?

Ben Garlic. It used to be thought to ward off evil spirits.

Tim This is getting more and more like one of those old Hammer movies. We shall have Christopher Lee appearing at any moment. Hey, where did you get this? (*He holds up the Familiar*)

Ben Meg gave it to Diana.

Tim Meg did?

Ben She said it was a Familiar, I believe. Some sort of local good luck charm. Isn't it?

Tim Yes, we sold dozens. I didn't know there were any left. I thought they'd all gone, years ago. It's a replica of one of those gargoyle things from the church. You wouldn't believe how superstitious these country people can be. My dear fellow, you're not taking this seriously, are you? The Wychcombe Familiar is just a piece of local folk-lore. Godfrey resurrected it to raise some cash. You can't be suggesting that we have an active coven, operating here in the village?

Ben Of course not. The garlic and the swastika are obviously someone's idea of a joke. A pretty poor one, I grant you, but still a joke.

Tim Well there you are then.

Ben My problem is that Diana doesn't see it as a joke. She is genuinely frightened. Then, to make matters worse, she found a dead rat in here just now.

Tim A dead rat, you're joking!

Ben No. It was here all right, the cat must have brought it in. Diana was terrified.

Tim Yes. I'm with her there. Can't bear rats, dead or alive. Did you know they used to build them into the walls in old houses?

Ben No, why?

Tim Well, a bit like the Familiar, to ward off the ghosties and ghoulies. As I said, superstition.

Ben Unfortunately, Diana believes that it's all part of an evil campaign aimed at her personally, and that Jessy Beer is behind it. I've been unable to convince her otherwise.

Tim Jessy Beer? Why on earth would Jessy Beer ——?

Ben Exactly. Why would Jessy Beer, or anyone else be trying to scare Diana out of her wits? Besides, to put it tactfully, I rather doubt that Jessy would be capable of hatching such a plot.

Tim I wouldn't be too sure about that.

Ben No?

Tim According to Meg, Jessy is by no means as dim as she makes out. She just likes you to think she is.

Ben Why?

Tim It's a-well established game, to fool the incomers. The locals get one hell of a kick out of playing village idiots. Amuses them no end.

Ben Incomers?

Tim That's you and me, old chum. I've lived here ever since Meg and I were married, but I'm still an incomer. The locals have subtle ways of reminding you. For instance they still ring up and ask for Meg Parkhouse. Meg's maiden name. No, according to Meg, Jessy Beer is both clever and cunning.

Ben What makes Meg say that?

Tim God knows, old boy. Women's intuition I dare say, and you can't argue with that. Though I will say, Meg's usually right about people.

Ben Well I can't tackle Jessy on the evidence of women's intuition, can I? But for the sake of Diana's peace of mind, I must find out who is responsible, and why.

Tim As I see it. You have a choice. You can ignore the whole thing. That way, the trickster will soon stop. Spoil their fun. Eh? Or, you could go to the police.

Ben The police! Good heavens, I can't do that. I should be had up for wasting their time, and suppose the press got hold of it — it's just the sort of publicity the Church doesn't need. Besides, it would finish Diana. As you can imagine, we had to deal with a lot of press attention when David died.

Tim Tell you what. If you get any more trouble, let me know. There's a police inspector at the golf club. Don't know him well, but I could have a quiet word, strictly off the record. Let's see what happens, eh? (*He stands*)

Ben Well thank you. It's good of you to come; I'm keeping you from your dinner, I'm sure.

Tim Nothing special. It's WI night, so that means something festering in the bottom of the Aga. Don't bother, old chap, I can see myself out. (*He moves to the door*)

Diana enters. She has her coat over her arm and is carrying an umbrella

Diana Good-evening.

Tim Hallo there. Are you off to the jam session too?

Diana Jam session? Oh, I see what you mean — actually it's Thai cookery this evening, I think.

Tim How adventurous. Don't know how the good yeoman of Wychcombe are going to take to that for their "bit o' dinner". 'Bye, both of you.

Tim exits

Diana So, what did you two decide between you? To have me committed and Jessy canonized?

Ben That's too childish for words, I'm not going to answer that.

Diana Sorry. So what was his solution?

Ben To ignore the whole thing. He thinks that whoever is responsible will give up once they see they can't rattle us. I think that's pretty sound ——

Diana In other words, he agrees with you. Do nothing, and hide behind the sofa till it's nice again. (*She puts her coat on*)

Ben You going somewhere?

Diana Yes, I'm going to a WI meeting with Meg.

Ben Are you sure you feel up to it? Perhaps you'd be better to have an early night; you could watch the television and I could bring you up some ...

Diana Oh for God's sake Ben, I'm not ill!

Ben Darling, I didn't say you were, but ——

Diana (*shouting*) Then for pity's sake, when are you going to stop treating me as if I were some demented madwoman?

Ben (*shouting back*) When you stop acting like one.

They both look aghast

Oh, Di, listen to us. What's happening to us?

Diana It's this place.

Ben Wychcombe?

Diana Perhaps, certainly this house, there's something about it.

Ben Oh, darling, there can't be. We agreed, it has no history.

Diana Then we were wrong, can't you feel it? It's built on evil.

Ben says nothing; he knows it would be pointless to argue. Diana picks up her bag and umbrella and goes towards the hall door. She turns

I hoped everything would be different here.

Ben It will be. You'll see.

Diana No. It's followed us. Perhaps it isn't the house, perhaps it's us. We've brought our own history with us. We shall never be able to escape it.

The church bell starts to toll erratically like an alarm signal

Ben What on earth ... ?
Diana The bell again.
Ben This time I'll find out who. I must dash.
Diana I'll come with you: one of us round the front, the other round ——
Ben No! Stay here.
Diana But I don't want to be here on my own. Please ——
Ben No! Ring Tim, tell him to meet me at the church.

Ben dashes out

The bell stops. Diana goes to the phone and puts in the numbers. There is a delay while the phone is answered

Diana (*into the phone*) Meg? Oh, thank God you're there. Where's Tim ? ... Well he should be, any moment. ... He's just left here. ... Yes. ...Goodness knows! ... Ben's on his way down to the church; as soon as he comes in, ask Tim to meet Ben at the church.

Diana puts down the phone and stands there, uncertain what to do

There is a banging on the window. Diana goes to the window and pulls back the curtain

Jessy is slumped against the window

Diana retreats in fear. Jessy manages to open the window and stagger a little way into the room. She is holding a gardening knife which she appears to be pointing at Diana. Diana is frozen with fear. Jessy staggers towards Diana, holding her arms out towards her and dropping the knife; she collapses against Diana, grasps her round the waist and then slowly slides to the floor down Diana's body. Diana is speechless with horror

Ben (*off*) Whoever it was gave me the slip, ring Tim and tell him not to bother.

Ben enters and sees Diana with Jessy at her feet

Di? What have you ...? Jessy?

Ben kneels beside Jessy and feels for a pulse in her neck. He takes his hand away and we see that it is covered in blood

CURTAIN

ACT II
SCENE 1

The same. Mid-morning the following Wednesday

When the CURTAIN *rises the room is empty*

We hear the doorbell

Ben enters from the kitchen, heading for the door to the hall

Ben (*calling*) I've put the kettle on. I'll just see who that is.

The phone rings. Ben, undecided which to answer first, picks up the phone

(*Into the phone*) Wychcombe Rectory, Ben Seaton here. ... No, I have no comment to make. ... My wife is not available. ... We neither of us wish to comment; thank you, goodbye.

Ben exits to the hall

Tim arrives outside the french windows and peers in. He is carrying a cardboard box tied up with string

Ben enters, sees the figure at the window and for a moment is startled. He opens the window

Tim Sorry to startle you, old chap. I did ring the doorbell.
Ben It was the telephone ... It's started I'm afraid — the press.
Tim Take the phone off the hook. (*He peers closely at Ben*) Everything all right, old chap? You looked a bit taken aback when you saw me just now.
Ben It's just, when I saw someone at the window — for a moment, I thought ... Jessy always came to the window.
Tim Aah. Dreadful business.
Ben Yes.
Tim Have the police said anything about how she died?
Ben Not really, you know what they're like.
Tim The word in the village is that she slit her own throat with a garden knife.
Ben That's how it seemed.

Tim Why ever would she have done it?

Ben In my experience, that's always an impossible question to answer ...
One thing: I realize I've forgotten to ask — is there anyone I should ...?
Did Jessy have any family?

Tim Not officially. Her mother died a year or two back.

Ben What do you mean, officially?

Tim Only local gossip, of course, but it's generally accepted in the village
that Jessy was related to the Rawlins family.

Ben You mean ...?

Tim Happens in the best of circles; it's just that in a village, it gets around.

Ben I see. Does Miss Rawlins know this?

Tim I'm sure she must. Godfrey Wheeler certainly did. Jessy's mother was
with him for years as a sort of housekeeper, and he made sure that Jessy had
steady employment, doing odd jobs around the rectory and the church.

Ben Do you mean that Godfrey Wheeler was —— ?

Tim Good God, no! Not him. Godfrey batted for the other side, as they say.
Local opinion favoured Em's brother, the one who was killed. Have you
got my wife here, old boy?

Ben She's upstairs with Diana. Very kind of Meg to come and sit with her.

Tim Not a bit of it. Doing me a favour. If she were at home she'd probably
while away the morning ripping out some perfectly serviceable fireplace.
How is Diana?

Ben Not too bad this morning, still a bit dazed. The doctor gave her a
knockout pill and she's been sleeping on and off ever since. She's only just
woken up. She seems surprisingly calm, but it's difficult to tell how much
of an effort she may be making. Shall I call Meg?

Tim Not for a bit. I take it the police will be here again.

Ben Yes, later this morning. I really don't know what more I can tell them.

Tim So you've told them everything that's been going on here?

Ben More or less ... I don't know what they made of it. I know I felt a
complete idiot going on about bells and angels and waving swastikas and
garlic at them. What have you got there?

Tim You'd better have a look.

Ben What is it?

Tim puts the box down and moves away. Ben opens the box and looks inside

Oh. Oh no! Oh dear, no. It's Felix.

Tim I'm sorry, old man.

Ben Poor, dear old Felix. What happened, was he run over?

Tim No.

Ben Where did you find him?

Tim In the church. Ben, I think you had better take a closer look.

Ben (*looking more closely*) Oh, dear God, who has done this? He's been strangled. The twine's still round his neck.

Tim I cut him down. He was hanging, in the belfry.

Ben gags and gets out his handkerchief. He goes to the window and turns away

Ben What kind of sick mind does a thing like this?

Tim I'm so sorry.

Ben He hasn't been in for a couple of days. We thought he must have gone walkabout, and all the time ... (*He blows his nose*) Poor dear old Felix — I can't ... He was — a good faithful old friend. We've been through a lot together, and to see him like that ... Excuse me. Why? For heaven's sake! Why?

Tim I don't know. You'll want to tell the police.

Ben Yes, yes, of course. What if Diana —— ?

Tim Look, don't worry, I'll pop off now, and take this with me, tell them I've got him in my garage.

Ben Thanks.

Tim I'll be back later. (*He picks up the box*)

Tim exits into the hall. We hear the front door opening, then Tim reappears with Emmeline Rawlins and Peter. Emmeline is carrying a book and Peter has some flowers

Found some callers on your doorstep, Ben.

Ben Come in, Miss Rawlins, Peter.

Tim 'Bye again.

Emmeline Timothy! I'm glad I bumped in to you. Would you kindly tell your workman not to park that van, with the deafening syncopated beat, outside my cottage?

Tim How do you know it's one of my workmen?

Emmeline You don't see many creatures with orange hair and rings in his ears, nose, eyebrows and God knows where else besides.

Tim Fair enough. Sounds like Damian.

Emmeline Damian! Whatever next? Just tell him, Timothy.

Tim I'll mention it, certainly, but I'm his employer, not his owner.

Tim exits into the hall

Emmeline I hope we're not intruding. We didn't know if we ought to bother you, it's difficult to know what to do. This is a dreadful thing to have happened, I can hardly believe it. We're so sorry, Mr Seaton, I heard that it was your wife who found ... Dreadful for her, poor girl. I thought she might like something to read. Take her mind off it. It's a history of this parish and our family. Just a little something my cousin Godfrey jotted down years ago. I promised to lend it to her. (*She hands the book to Ben*)

Ben That's really most kind of you, Miss Rawlins. I know she'll appreciate it.

Peter And I brought these for her. (*He hands the flowers to Ben*)

Ben That's most thoughtful ... (*He puts the presents down during the following*)

Peter Please just give her my regards. I can't stop actually. I must dash back and pack.

Ben You're leaving us?

Peter Yes, I'm off after lunch, my flight to Berlin is early evening.

Ben So we shan't be seeing you for a while?

Peter I'm in Berlin for the rest of this week and Milan and Barcelona next week. But after that, I'm hoping to get back for a long weekend next month. Well, goodbye Rector, it was nice meeting you. This tragic business with Jessy, it doesn't seem a very good start for a new parish, but I hope you and Mrs Seaton will not judge Wychcombe and its people too harshly. Coming, Auntie?

Emmeline You get on, I'll catch you up.

Peter See you back at the cottage. (*He makes for the door*)

Meg enters, meeting Peter

Meg Oh, sorry to barge in. Diana says has the kettle boiled yet?

Ben Ah, *mea culpa*, I got waylaid.

Peter Hi, Meg.

Meg Hallo Peter, you haven't been round to sniff my dry rot yet.

Peter No, just telling Mr Seaton here: I have a pretty busy time ahead for the next couple of weeks, but I'll call in when I'm next around.

Meg Good, see you then.

Peter exits into the hall

(*Making for the kitchen*) Right, I'll make some tea.

Meg exits into the kitchen

Ben looks enquiringly at Emmeline. It is obvious that she has something on her mind

Emmeline Mr Seaton. The book, that's not really why I came; it was just an excuse.

Ben I see. There was something else, then?

Emmeline It's about Jessy.

Ben In that case I don't think you should be telling me, Miss Rawlins, I think you should be telling the police.

Emmeline Well that's a bit difficult. Perhaps, if I told you the whole story, you might advise me as to how much I need tell the police.

Ben I see. Well, that depends on what you tell me.

Emmeline I think you should know that Jessy Beer was by no means as "simple" as she liked to make out. She is — she could be — scheming and manipulative.

Ben Certainly my wife found her—disturbing. But in what way manipulative?

Emmeline Mr Seaton, the first time we met, I told you about my other nephew, Frank Rawlins?

Ben Yes. I believe you brought them up, from small boys.

Emmeline Indeed I did, and a pretty poor job I made of it in Frank's case. It was ten years ago that he took part in the robbery. That night he turned up on my doorstep. I hadn't seen him for more than six years. He told me he was desperate and on the run. He stayed just long enough to eat, and collect all the cash I had in the house. The following morning the police came. I'm not proud of it, but I told them I hadn't seen him. As it was well known that we'd been estranged for years, they believed me.

Ben I see.

Emmeline It wouldn't have made any difference if I'd told them the truth; they picked him up later that day, miles away from here. I thought that would be the end of it, but a few days later Jessy Beer came to see me. It appeared that she had seen Frank leaving. She seemed to think that it would be worth my while to pay her to keep quiet about it.

Ben Blackmail?

Emmeline It was only small sums, and not on a regular basis. Just when she found herself short for the rent money. All the same, I came to dread her visits.

Ben I'm not surprised.

Emmeline For more than ten years, I thought I was paying Jessy to keep quiet about Frank's visit. On Sunday, for the first time, I realized that it was much worse than that.

Ben Worse? I don't understand.

Emmeline When she told me originally that she had seen Frank, all she said was, "I saw him leaving". Naturally, I assumed that she had seen him leaving my house, which would have been, oh, shortly after eleven p.m. On Sunday I realized for the first time that I had misunderstood her all these years.

Ben You mean she hadn't seen him?

Emmeline Oh yes, she saw him, but not when he left me, at elevenish. She claimed to have seen him, in his car, driving out of the village early the following morning.

Ben Forgive me, Miss Rawlins, but is the timing important?

Emmeline I'm afraid it is, Mr Seaton, because that was the morning, at around seven a.m., that the Taylor girl was run down. She was coming into the village to do her paper round.

Ben The same morning, and on the same road as Frank left Wychcombe?

Emmeline Now do you see? I heard what had happened to that poor little girl, of course, but until Sunday I had no reason to connect it with Frank, because as far as I was concerned he had left Wychcombe hours before. Now I find out that he didn't.

Ben But you can't be sure that Frank was responsible.

Emmeline No, but I'm afraid it all fits rather too neatly and Jessy seemed convinced that Frank had killed her.

Ben I can imagine how distressing this must be for you, Miss Rawlins.

Emmeline As I said, Jessy had only asked for small sums, previously. On Sunday she demanded a fairly large sum of money. She said she needed the money, because Mrs Seaton had poisoned your mind against her, and that you were about to sack her.

Ben That's not true. Although I have to admit that Diana was not entirely rational about it. Jessy frightened her badly, and Diana is convinced that she was doing it deliberately. However, there wasn't a shred of proof that Jessy set out to persecute her, and without proof I would never have sacked her.

Emmeline I think your wife's instincts may well have been right. Anyway, I lost my temper with her; I told her that she had gone too far and I had no intention of giving her another penny. I realized what I should have known all along: she would never have gone to the police. She would have had to explain why she had withheld vital evidence all these years.

Ben So, you are wondering if you should tell the police about Jessy's attempts to blackmail you?

Emmeline If I did, I should have to tell them about Frank's visit, and about his possible involvement in the Taylor girl's death. That would go even harder on Frank.

Ben I doubt whether they could prove anything after all this time, especially without Jessy as a witness. No, I think the blackmail is likely to be of more interest to them. You may not have been her only victim. I would like to wait a little while before I give an opinion, Miss Rawlins. There is something in the back of my mind that I would like to think about.

Emmeline By all means.

Ben If Jessy was telling the truth about seeing Frank at seven a.m. that morning, where do you think he might have spent the missing hours?

Emmeline I've racked my brains, Mr Seaton, and my best guess is that he went to the rectory to ask Godfrey for some more money. But if he did, Godfrey never mentioned it and that I do find strange. Even if Frank had sworn Godfrey to secrecy, everyone knew that Godfrey could never keep a secret. A sad failing in a priest, some might think!

Ben Miss Rawlins, do you know in which prison your nephew is being held? Because, if you're going to tell the police, he ought to be warned.

Emmeline Frank was released on parole, earlier this year. Since then, I understand that he has not been seen. The police came to see me, a few weeks ago, to know if I had any idea of his whereabouts. It hurt me a great deal to have to admit that I have neither seen him nor heard from him. You see, Mr Seaton, whatever he has done, I still love him dearly, and I always will.

Ben When did you last see him?

Emmeline To speak to? The evening of the robbery. I was in court every day, of course, during his trial, and after, I tried to keep in touch with him, but he refused to see me, or answer any of my letters. It broke my heart, but in the end I just had to accept his wishes. Even now, part of me has never give up hope. In fact — Mr Seaton, do you believe in premonition?

Ben How do you mean? Like second sight?

Emmeline I'm not sure. I don't know the words to describe it, but — just recently, I have had this feeling ... I just know that I shall see him soon. Frank is coming home, Mr Seaton. I know it. After all the years, Frank is coming home.

Ben I hope so, Miss Rawlins.

Emmeline Thank you for your time, Rector. You will let me know what you think?

Ben I'll ring you tomorrow.

Ben and Emmeline exit to the hall. Tim pokes his head round the kitchen door then enters

We hear a murmur from the hall as Emmeline leaves

Ben returns

Tim All clear? Em gone?

Ben Yes.

Tim Thank God for that! What did she want, or was it confidential?

Ben Sort of. Tim, did you know Frank Rawlins?

Tim Not well. I've met him several times, of course — oh, must be twenty years ago, through Meg. As I told you, they've known each other since childhood.

Ben What did you make of him?

Tim Frank? Oh, he can charm the birds off the trees. Dashing, plausible as the devil, but totally unreliable. What you have to understand is, that by the time he was ten years old, Frank had lost everything — parents, home, status. Hate to say it, but Em made him what he is. She brought him up to think of himself as the young squire, but that had all gone. So, as far as Frank is concerned, the world owes him a living.

Ben But didn't that rub off on Peter, too?

Tim He wasn't the heir. You'd have thought Peter might have resented that. Wouldn't you? You know, so near and yet so far. But there, different character altogether. You wouldn't expect them to have been so different, would you? Chalk and cheese. Poles apart, I've never understood it.

Ben The gang he was with, did they all get long sentences?

Tim They never caught the others and they never recovered any of the loot. Frank went down all by himself.

Meg and Diana enter

Ben Hallo, darling. You're all dressed. How are you feeling?

Diana Much better.

Meg My mother always reckoned that if you were feeling a bit under, the best tonic was to dress up and put on your slap.

The phone rings. Ben answers it

Ben (*into the phone*) The Rectory, Ben ... Please don't ring again. ... I have nothing to say. ... You're wasting your time, and mine. ... Good-day! (*He hangs up*)

Diana Papers?

Ben nods

Meg has a suggestion to make. Tell them, Meg.

Meg Yes, well, we've been hatching up a little scheme.

Tim Bound to be expensive.

Meg I thought it might do Diana good to get away from here for a while.

Tim Thought so. I told you.

Meg On the contrary. It won't cost a penny. Tim's sister has a holiday cottage in Wales. It's a beautiful spot, so peaceful, miles from anywhere. We have an invitation to use it at any time.

Ben It might be the best thing at the moment. This is going to get worse. (*He indicates the phone*) Would you like to go, darling?

Diana Oh yes, could we, Ben?

Ben When?

Diana This evening? Tomorrow?

Ben That soon? Well — I suppose ——

Diana Please, Ben.

Ben If the police say it's all right to leave — but I'd have to be back for the weekend.

Meg We'd thought of that. I could drive down on Saturday and stay on for a while with Diana. I'll drive her back sometime next week.

Ben But we couldn't impose.

Meg I should enjoy it. I've been meaning to go down there for ages. It's a solidly-built stone cottage but it needs modernizing. She could do with my advice.

Tim Oh, in that case, go with my blessing! I'm all for it. You can dream up ways of spending Sis's money instead of mine.

Meg Then it's settled. I'll ring Mrs Price straight away — she's the old girl who looks after the place. I'll tell her to expect you this evening?

Diana Oh, what about Felix? Who will feed Felix?

Ben and Tim exchange awkward glances

Meg Don't worry, I'll come in and feed him till Ben gets back.

Diana Thank you. That reminds me, he hasn't been in for his breakfast yet. I'll just go and call him.

Diana exits to the kitchen

Ben I must make some phone calls — Miss Rawlins first. (*He goes to the phone, looks up the number and dials. Into the phone*) Miss Rawlins? ... Ben Seaton here. ... Look, something has come up, and we shall be away for a few days. ... Yes, leaving this evening. We'll have a chat when I get back. ... Goodbye. (*He hangs up*)

Wild screams are heard from Diana in the kitchen. Diana rushes in

Ben What is it, what's happened?

Diana rushes into Ben's arms and cowers there

Diana The door, the back door.

Tim I'll go.

Tim exits into the kitchen

Ben tries to calm Diana who is whimpering

Tim enters. He is carrying a crude-looking doll with a hideous face, a noose round its neck and knitting needles sticking into it

Tim It was hanging on the back door. I'll swear it wasn't there ten minutes ago — I came round that way.

Ben Look, Diana, it's just a doll, that's all it is, just a rag doll.

Diana But she's gone, Jessy's dead ...

Meg Let me see.

Tim hands the doll to Meg, who holds it in front of her, a smile spreading across her face

Well, well, so that's it.
Tim Meg? What?
Meg (*holding the doll towards Diana*) He's right. It's only a doll.

Diana screams, backs away in horror and falls into a dead faint

CURTAIN

SCENE 2

The same. Wednesday evening. 7 p.m.

When the CURTAIN *rises there is a gale blowing outside and the wind is howling. A fire is burning in the grate*

Diana is standing by the window staring listlessly out into the darkness

Ben enters from the hall. He is wearing an overcoat and carrying Diana's coat

Ben Here you are darling, better put this on. It's quite nippy outside in this storm.
Diana Funny, we never did decide where to put the roses.
Ben No, well plenty of time for that when we get back, eh?
Diana Perhaps we shouldn't go — perhaps we shan't come back.
Ben That's silly, Diana; it was your idea ——
Diana I know, but I have this feeling. If we leave this house now, we'll never come back, I'm sure of it.
Ben I'm not going to argue, Diana, it's all arranged. The lady who looks after the cottage has got food in and turned on the heating. She'll wait there till we arrive.

Meg enters with Diana's suitcase

Meg There, I hope I've remembered everything, Diana. Not that you'll need much. Rural Wales isn't exactly social.
Diana Thank you, Meg, I'm sure it's fine.
Meg If there's anything I've forgotten you can let me know, and I'll bring it with me on Saturday.
Diana Yes, of course. But why rush? We could go in the morning. Look at you, Ben, you're tired out after all that time with the police. And I'm not sure it's safe to drive in this gale. Ring Mrs ... whatever her name is ...

Meg Mrs Price.

Diana Ring her and say we'll come down in the morning.

Meg Can't get hold of her. She'll be at the cottage and there's no phone. Mrs Price is not the sort to have a mobile.

Ben Diana, please, love, Tim's arranged it all. We can't change things now, it's too late.

Diana Too late — yes. That's what I'm afraid of.

Ben Diana, please!

Diana We can't keep running away.

Ben It isn't running away. It's only for a few days. I've told everyone I'll be back on Saturday.

Diana You will, but if I walk out of this house, I'm not sure I'll ever have the courage to walk back in again.

Ben Than we'll just have to cross that bridge when we come to it. I'll take these things out to the car. I'll be back for you in a minute. The sooner we get started, the sooner we'll be there.

Ben exits with the suitcase

Meg Don't worry, Diana. I'll lock up and see to everything.

Diana What about Felix? Suppose he comes home and neither of us is here?

Meg I'll keep an eye out for him, I promise. I'll come over every day and leave food.

Diana You don't think he's going to come back, do you? I can see it in your eyes.

Meg Diana, maybe he has just gone walkabout, but — you must face the possibility that something's happened to him. This is the country, things happen. Farms can be dangerous places — machinery, poison — lots of things. Foxes, perhaps.

Diana Yes. Poor Felix. He was David's cat, you know. He arrived at Christmas when David was five years old. He was our last link ——

Ben enters

Ben All ready?

Diana nods

Good. Off we go then.

Diana I haven't left a note for the milkman.

Meg I'll see to everything, you mustn't worry.

Ben takes Diana to the door

Ben 'Bye, Meg. Thanks for everything.

Meg Relax, have a rest, try to forget things for a while. See you Friday.

*Ben and Diana exit, followed by Meg. We hear more goodbyes in the hall
and the sound of the front door closing; and in a little while, a car drives
away. Meg enters*

*Meg plumps up the cushions, settles the fire and puts the guard in front. She
opens the window then realizes that she can't lock it as there is no key. She
gives a little grunt of satisfaction and pulls the curtains*

Meg exits to the kitchen and enters with an empty milk bottle

*Meg goes to the desk, scribbles a note and sticks it in the top of the milk bottle.
The Lights go out, leaving just enough light from the fire for Meg to see her
way across the room. She gives a gasp of alarm and heads for the door. She
has just reached the door when the Lights give a flicker and come on again.
She turns them off*

Meg exits to the kitchen

We hear the back door slam

*By the dim light of the fire, we see Meg enter, softly closing the kitchen door
behind her. She tiptoes to the window and peeps carefully out of the side
of the curtain. She goes to the sofa and settles down to wait*

*There is a Black-out to denote the passing of half an hour. Meg closes her eyes
and apparently dozes off*

Slowly the dim firelight is restored

*There is a noise at the window. Meg's eyes fly open. She moves swiftly and
silently to the light switch*

*The curtains part and Peter, dressed all in black, slips into the room with
a torch*

*Peter closes the curtains behind him and then switches on his torch. He goes
to the desk and opens the drawer where the plans are kept. Meg switches on
the lights and Peter spins to face her*

Peter Meg!
Meg Make sure those curtains are tightly closed and switch on the desk lamp.

Peter does what he is told

Peter Meg, what are you doing here?

Meg turns off the main light

Meg I might ask you the same question. I'm locking up for the Seatons. What's your excuse?

Peter I thought you'd left by the back door ——

Meg That's what you were supposed to think. I guessed you'd be out there somewhere.

Peter How very clever of you. (*He glances nervously towards the window*)

Meg Don't worry, we shan't be disturbed. The Seatons are speeding their way towards Wales and Tim's gone to a parish council meeting. He'll think I'm home by now.

Peter I see. You seem to have gone to a lot of trouble to arrange all this. May I ask why?

Meg I wanted to see you. Why have you been playing these infantile, occult pranks on the Seatons?

Peter How do you know it was me?

Meg I didn't at first, until I saw that obscene doll. That was careless of you. It may have been thirty plus years ago, but you don't think I've forgotten the Wychcombe coven, do you?

Peter Of course. The jolly old Wychcombe coven. Shame on me, you're right, that was careless. I'd forgotten you were part of it too.

Meg Huh! When I think what a thrill it was for me, to be allowed to play with the Rawlins boys, in the rectory garden, and you didn't even remember I was there. Now why doesn't that surprise me? The coven was our favourite game. The two of you took it in turns to be the wicked priest, Sir Basil Rawlins, or the witch catcher. I was the village maiden in Sir Basil's thrall. We'd excommunicate Sir Basil with bell, book and candle then burn him at the stake whilst he screamed satanic curses upon our heads.

Peter Happy days. And they say that modern children are sophisticated. So how did you know it was me? It could just as easily have been Frank.

Meg Just as easily. In fact, it took me some while to puzzle it out. Was it Peter? Or was it Frank? Or were you both involved?

Peter And what conclusion did you come to?

Meg The first moment I saw you, on Sunday, I couldn't help noticing the way you looked at me. It flashed across my mind that — but I dismissed the idea. Told myself I had imagined it. But it kept coming back. I remembered how you used to change places as boys. Do you remember old Miss Jarvis? Who taught Sunday School? I remembered how the two of you used to play her up. She called you limbs of Satan, and used to march the pair of you into the rector, and demand to know which was which, and sometimes, even he wasn't sure.

Peter My, what a long memory you have, Meg. So have you finally decided? Me or my twin? (*He laughs*)

Meg Oh, yes, I've decided, once I heard about the cat, it wasn't difficult. That had your mark stamped all over it. Only you would have been capable of such casual cruelty.

Peter Oh, come on, Meg, you're a farmer's daughter, you never used to so squeamish.

Meg What's it all for, Frank?

Peter I would have thought that someone with your remarkable powers of deduction would have worked that out already.

Meg You wanted the Seatons out of the house.

Peter Full marks!

Meg And where did Jessy come into all this?

Peter Jessy was very useful. I had to pay her of course, but I really think she would have put the frighteners on poor little Diana Seaton for nothing, she enjoyed it so much. Remarkable woman, Jessy, mine of information. I found out she knew that I'd been here in Wychcombe on the night of the robbery.

Meg She told you?

Peter No. I overheard her trying to blackmail Aunt Em. Apparently Aunt Em had been paying up for years. This time Jessy wanted a lot more.

Meg What did Miss Rawlins say?

Peter She told Jessy to go to hell, or words to that effect. I'd never seen Auntie so riled. She tore into Jessy.

Meg I'm glad she told Jessy her fortune. I wish I'd had the courage.

Peter Courage? Oh no, she was blackmailing you, too?

Meg She knew we'd spent that night together. She saw you leave Miss Rawlins' cottage and come straight to me. She knew Tim was away during the week.

Peter laughs

What's funny?

Peter Poor old Tim, even he should appreciate the irony of this situation. If he ever found out.

Meg Irony?

Peter You've been paying Jessy with Tim's cash, all these years, just to protect his peace of mind.

Meg What else would you have expected me to do?

Peter Knowing you, Meg, exactly what you did. You're not the type to let a fling with an old flame stand in the way of you becoming the new lady of the manor.

Meg You make me sick. You're just like the rest of your tribe.

Peter My tribe?

Meg The Rawlins; people like you. Even as children, you and Peter never had any doubts. You were born with the effortless confidence of superiority.

Peter Surely you aren't accusing us of snobbery?

Meg Of course not. Snobbery is for those with social aspirations. The Rawlins don't need to aspire to anything, why should they? Take your aunt, she'd still be gentry, even if she lived in a slum. It would never occur to her to doubt that.

Peter Very revealing. Do all the locals despise us as you do?

Meg I don't despise you, I never have. Envy you perhaps.

Peter Envy us? But you're Meg Bestwood, wife of a rich man. What have we got that you could possibly envy?

Meg You would never understand. For a farmer's daughter, a place in the sun has to be earned. For the likes of the Rawlins, it's their birthright, even when they haven't two pennies to rub together.

Peter (*laughing again*) I was just thinking, what an absurd time to be having a debate on the class system.

Meg I agree. You still haven't told me what this is all about. Why did you come here?

Peter All in good time.

Meg And why were you pretending to be Peter?

Peter I had to. The truth of the matter is, I'm in a bit of trouble. Since I got out, I've been lying low.

Meg But why? Why do you have to lie low? Who are you in trouble with, the police?

Peter Only indirectly. Let's say that both the police and my former colleagues would give a lot to know where I am.

Meg Why? What colleagues?

Peter My mates. Partners in crime. There were two others in on that bullion raid, besides me. We worked on the assumption that since I had no serious criminal record, the police were unlikely to connect me with the raid. Ha! How wrong can you be? Anyway, the plan was, that I should stash the loot and then fade into the background. Then later, we would meet up and divide the spoils. It didn't go according to plan. I was the one they arrested. The other two have been waiting ten long years to find out what happened to their share.

Meg And that's why you're in hiding?

Peter I knew that once I was released, my every move would be watched by the police and the other two. From day one of my arrest I had a cunning plan, as they say, I cut off all contact with the family. I refused to see Aunt Em or communicate in any way. With none of the loot recovered I knew they would be monitoring my visitors, and screening phone calls and letters. I made sure I had none.

Meg But even if nobody bothered to watch Miss Rawlins, or Peter? Surely, this is still the first place they would think of looking for you?

Peter Which was why I had to pretend to be Peter. That gave me a free hand to recover the gold whenever I liked.

Meg But what about the other two? Isn't there supposed to be honour, even among thieves?

Peter Oh, please, I did ten years for that stuff while they were on the outside, living the life of Riley. In my opinion, ten years cancels any debt of honour. You know, when you first stuck your nose in, Meg, I was a bit alarmed, but now I see how we can turn it to our advantage.

Meg I don't see how.

Peter Because you're going to help me.

Meg Help you!

Peter Of course you will. Think, Meg, with all that money, we can get out of the country, make a new life for ourselves.

Meg We can?

Peter Don't tell me you haven't thought about it, Meg. From our teenage years, when we used to meet down in Dingly Dell, can you honestly say that it's ever been better for you? It's never been better for me, I know that. And you saw it in my eyes when we met, you said you did. You and I were always meant to be together, you know that. But life got in our way. I screwed up and you married Tim. But think, it's not too late, we're being given a second chance.

Meg (*looking at him in disbelief*) You're really serious, aren't you?

Peter Never more so. That night I came to you, when I was on the run, I told you then how much I needed you. I still need you, I always will. You must help me get the stuff. It's for us, and then we can be together, just the two of us, and damn the rest of the world.

Meg You say get the stuff — from where?

Peter Oh, Meg, I'm disappointed in you. Haven't you guessed? It's here, right here.

Meg Here?

Peter Of course, where else? Before I dropped in on Aunt Em that night, I stopped off and buried the box in Uncle Godfrey's garden. Right in the heart of dear old Dingly Dell. In the shrubbery.

Meg The shrubbery? But that's — here — here, under this house. Frank, face facts, it's lost! It's lost forever. (*She laughs*)

Peter (*hysterically*) Stop that!

Meg stops and looks at him warily

Now you see why I had to get the Seatons out of the house.

Meg But what good is it going to do?

Peter Listen! (*From here on his manner becomes wilder*) After I'd given the
police and my mates the slip, I came down here to dig it up. Christ! Can you
imagine? They'd only built a bloody house over it. I told myself, don't
panic, do your homework, find out all you can about the enemy.

Meg The enemy?

Peter I read in the local paper that they'd appointed a new rector. So I nipped
up to his old parish and genned up on the family history. After that, I was
able to plan a campaign and frighten them out. It was child's play.

Meg It was inhuman.

Peter Mind you, I had some anxious moments. Finding a suitable grave was
the most fantastic luck, until I found out that Jessy knew I'd run over that
Taylor kid.

Meg Oh no! Oh God!

Peter It wasn't my fault, it was an accident. I didn't mean to kill her. The silly
kid was walking along the side of the road in the dark. I didn't even see her
until it was too late. Just my bad luck.

Meg You're crazy.

Peter Don't say that! Don't ever say that.

Meg Frank, listen to me. This has gone too far. Tell the police where the gold
is hidden and ask for their protection.

Peter Ha! Ha! Now who's crazy?

Meg But that gold isn't yours, it never was.

Peter Then who does it belong to, eh? Answer me that. (*Ranting*) The bank?
Don't be naïve, they settled for the insurance money years ago. The
Treasury? They steal every day. They stole Wychcombe Hall from me. It
wasn't theirs to take. It was ours. The Rawlins had lived there for
generations. It was our inheritance.

Meg Frank, that's mad.

Peter Mad, is it? I'll show you who's mad. If we don't have it, nobody will.

Meg But you can't dig up a whole house!

Peter (*triumphantly*) We won't have to. Look. (*He takes out the plans and
lays them over the table behind the sofa*) See, here. Come and take a look,
Meg. There! Now tell me that isn't the luck of the Rawlins. By my
calculations, it's right there, just where Mrs Seaton was going to plant her
roses. Another five feet and — Meg! Don't be a spoilsport, come and take
a look.

Meg goes over reluctantly and leans over the plans

(*Tracing features on the map with his finger*) Look, here is the
boundary fence, you remember? The wicket gate is still there and so is
this oak tree ——

Peter raises the other arm and brings the heavy torch down on Meg's head. Meg slumps forward and slides to the floor behind the sofa. Peter kneels by her to make sure she really is out cold

Peter exits to the kitchen and comes back knotting two tea towels together

Peter kneels down beside Meg once more and loops the knotted tea towels around her neck. We see him strain to strangle Meg

There is a sound outside the window. Peter hears this and rises quickly, turns out the desk lamp and flattens himself at the side of the window

Emmeline (*off*) Frank? (*Softly*) Frank? Is that you dear?

Emmeline enters through the curtains

Don't be afraid, dear, it's me, Auntie Em, and I'm not cross. Let's talk about this, Frank. (*She moves to the centre of the room*)

There is a noise from outside the window. Emmeline hears it and turns to the window. Peter turns the beam of the torch full in Emmeline's face

Oh, there you are dear. I knew it was you. I've been waiting for you. I saw you come in through the window a little while ago. I watched until the coast was clear and then I came over. What are you doing here, Frank? You shouldn't be here, you know, dear. Frank, turn the light away, please. It's hurting my eyes.

Peter turns out the torch

That's better. Let me see you, dear.

Peter turns on the desk lamp

Peter Hallo, Auntie.
Emmeline Now we have lots to talk about, dear. Peter was here. Did you know? You just missed him, he left this afternoon. What a pity; we could have had the family together for the first time for ... Oh, and there have been some very strange things happening, Jessy Beer is dead and it seems she ——
Peter What are you wittering on about, you senile old fool?
Emmeline Frank, dear, what are you saying ——?
Peter Auntie, Auntie Em, look at me. Peter hasn't been here, I have.

Emmeline You have, but why? Why have you been pretending to be Peter?
Peter I had to Auntie; I did it for us, for the family.
Emmeline I don't understand, what did you do? That wasn't you, was it?
Was it? Trying to frighten the Seatons? I thought it was Jessy.
Peter Jessy, huh! I got rid of them, didn't I? They don't really belong here,
you know that.

*Emmeline may be blinkered in the case of Frank but she recognizes that he
is unbalanced and from now on shows some wariness*

Emmeline But Frank, things have changed, you've been away for a long
time.

Meg moans. Emmeline turns and sees her

Good heavens! Meg? What has happened? What have you done to Meg?
Peter I haven't done anything to her. She's fainted. (*He goes and kneels
beside Meg, blocking Em's view with his body and removes the tea towels
from Meg's neck*)
Emmeline I don't believe you, something's happened.
Peter Don't be ridiculous, Auntie, see for yourself. (*He straightens up and
swiftly slips the improvised noose behind the sofa cushion*)

Emmeline kneels down by Meg. Frank raises the torch

Ben enters from the hall and turns on the main lights

Ben What on earth? Good-evening Miss Rawlins, and Sir Francis — it is Sir
Francis, isn't it?
Peter Just Frank will do.
Ben Right, Frank. I don't want to seem inhospitable, but may I ask what you
are doing here?
Emmeline Oh, please, Mr Seaton. Thank goodness you're here. Something
has happened to Meg.
Ben Meg! Whatever ... Meg?
Emmeline Help me get her on to the sofa.

Emmeline and Ben half-lift, half-support Meg to the sofa

Ben There's a nasty bang on her head. What has been going on, Miss
Rawlins?
Emmeline I don't know. I've just arrived; they were already here.
Ben (*to Meg*) Meg — Meg, can you hear me? (*To Emmeline*) I'd better ring
for a doctor.

Emmeline (*quickly*) No!

Ben No?

Emmeline I mean, look, she's nearly come round.

Ben Good. Meg, can you hear me? How did this happen?

Peter I was just explaining to Auntie: she fainted. She must have caught her head as she fell.

Ben Fainted? How did she come to faint?

Peter I think it would be better if I spoke to you in private, Mr Seaton.

Ben No need for that, surely?

Peter Very well, as you please. It's just that — it's rather — delicate.

Ben Delicate, I see.

Peter Mrs Bestwood, Meg, asked me to meet her here. She thought you had gone to Wales, and would not be back tonight.

Ben My wife was taken ill, we had to turn back. Why did Mrs Bestwood ask you to meet her here?

Peter Please, Mr Seaton. Meg and I are old friends — perhaps we should leave it at that.

Emmeline That can't be true. Meg would never ... That was all over years ago.

Peter Auntie, please! You don't know what you are talking about. Enough has been said.

Ben Yes. Perhaps we should leave it at that for now. You've been looking at the plans of the house, I see. It's a very well-built house, I'm told. Especially solid foundations. Solid gold, one might say.

Peter I'm sorry? I don't quite follow you.

Ben You don't? I'm speaking of buried treasure. Most exciting, don't you think?

Peter Buried treasure?

Ben I've every reason to think so. Solid gold bars.

Peter A divine revelation?

Ben Hardly, more of an educated guess. Am I warm?

Peter Just about spot on, I should say. I'm impressed.

Ben It wasn't that difficult. When I found out that you had been here for some hours that night, the night of the robbery ——

Peter You found out? Who told you? Only three people knew, and I made sure ——

Ben It doesn't matter how I found out, but I realized that someone was trying to frighten us out of the house to get at the gold. But who? You were the obvious candidate, of course. But nobody seemed to know where you were. It did occur to me that you might be in hiding somewhere around here, and that Peter was helping you. Then, this afternoon the last piece of the puzzle fell into place. Tim made a reference to the fact that you and your brother are identical twins. I had no idea, and amazingly, no-one had mentioned it. Just assumed that I knew, I suppose. I was now nearly certain

I knew how it had been done. A transatlantic phone call, to a rather surprised Dr Peter Rawlins in California, confirmed it.

Meg tries to struggle up. She clasps her throat

Peter Well, not much more to say, is there? Game, set and match to you, Rector. I think I'll just slip away quietly, and leave you in peace.
Ben There's still the little matter of the bullion.
Peter I hadn't forgotten. In fact, I think we can do a deal about that. I'll tell you where to find it, and you tell the bank. They're still offering a reward for information leading to the recovery of the gold. I'm sure you can put the money to good use — the church roof, or the tower; there's always something needing repair.
Ben Are you suggesting that in exchange for the reward money, I should allow you to just walk out of here?
Peter I rather doubt if you could stop me. Bye, Auntie, look after yourself.

Peter goes to the french windows and pulls back the curtain

Tim is in the doorway, barring Peter's exit

Tim Hallo Frank, long time no see. Are you leaving us, old boy?
Peter I am.
Tim I don't think so, old chap. There are a few people out here who are just waiting for you to make a run for it.
Peter Waiting for me?
Tim That's right, the boys in blue. They've been surrounding the house ever since you entered it. Never seen such to-ing and fro-ing as we've had here tonight. I don't know where it's more crowded, inside or out. Oh, by the way, they've got a warrant for your arrest.
Emmeline What!
Peter On what charge?
Tim Murder of course, old chap, what else?
Emmeline Murder!

During the following Peter shrinks back against Emmeline as if for protection

Tim The murder of Jessy Beer.
Peter But Jessy committed suicide.
Tim Oh no. The police knew from the start that she'd been murdered.

Meg leans back against the sofa cushion and feels something. She pulls the knotted tea towels from behind the cushion

Peter This is a frame-up. Don't listen to them, Auntie. They've no evidence. Why should I kill Jessy?

Tim We were hoping you might tell us.

Peter There, do you see? They're bluffing.

Meg I can tell you.

Tim Meg — Meg, what are you doing here, I thought you were ... (*He moves to Meg*)

Meg I'll explain later. Jessy was ——

Peter Shut up, Meg! I'm warning you.

Meg It's too late, Frank. He killed Jessy to silence her. He found out that Jessy saw him, here in Wychcombe, after the robbery. He tried to kill me for the same reason. (*She holds out the knotted tea towels*)

Peter It's a lie. Auntie, tell them she's lying. She's trying to cover up for herself.

Meg Not any more.

Tim You knew that Frank had been here, Meg? How did you know?

Meg Because he came to see me that night. You were away.

Tim Oh. Oh, I see.

Emmeline Oh, Frank — Frank.

Peter (*to Emmeline, urgently*) Auntie, look at me, listen to me, you've got to believe me. I had to kill Jessy, she left me no choice. You can see that. She was blackmailing you, she was going to give me away, ruin our chances. (*He sinks to his knees and grasps both of Emmeline's hands. His breath becomes more laboured*) You wouldn't have wanted that. You know how you always loved me best. You used to call me your best boy. I did it all for the family, for you ...

Diana enters through the french windows and watches the following

Emmeline Shh, Frank. Breathe deeply, my dear, stay calm. Don't say any more.

Peter No, Auntie. I'm quite calm — I can't breathe ——

Emmeline Yes, you can dear. Now, get up, there's a good boy.

Frank rises

That's better. Come along, dear, take my hand.

Emmeline leads Peter to the french windows like a small child

Come with me, Frank, dear, we'll go and explain.

Peter That's right, Auntie. You can explain. They'll listen to you.

Diana stands aside to allow Emmeline and Peter to pass

(*Turning solicitously to Diana; politely*) Good-evening, Mrs Seaton. I hope you are quite recovered.

Emmeline and Peter exit

Diana stays by the window during the following

Diana What will happen to him?

Tim After that performance I'd guess he's aiming at Broadmoor.

Ben You think he was putting it on?

Tim She wasted her money sending him to Sandhurst; he should have gone to RADA.

Ben Diana, are you all right? I told you to stay in the car.

Diana It was getting cold.

Meg (*to Diana*) When did you know? That they'd arranged this little charade between them?

Diana Just outside the village Ben turned the car, and explained why we were going back.

Tim Sorry, old thing, I should have told you, but we never for one moment expected you to barge in here like you did.

Meg (*quietly*) No, I don't suppose you did. You see ——

Tim Shh ... We'll talk later. We ought to get you home, my dear, you've had a rough evening.

Meg (*looking at him uncertainly*) Home?

Tim Of course. Where else would we go?

Meg takes Tim's hand and bites her lip to hold back the tears

Meg Poor old Em — and poor Frank. His life could have been so different.

Tim Come on. Let me give you a hand. Cheer up, old thing (*Tenderly, he wipes the tears from her cheeks*) I know, think of tomorrow.

Tim leads Meg towards the hall

They're coming to move the Aga and rip out all the old pipes. That's something to look forward to, now isn't it?

They exit. Ben follows them out

Diana moves to the desk and leans over it with her back to the room

Ben enters

Ben I'm sorry I had to spring all this on you, but the police seemed to think that the fewer people who knew about it, the better. Our departure had to be convincing. (*He rakes the fire into life*)

Diana It certainly convinced me.

Ben Are you warm enough? Shall I make some tea?

Diana No milk.

Ben No, of course. Tell you what, let's drink the dregs of the Christmas sherry, that's if Tim has left us any. (*He pours two glasses of sherry and hands Diana one*)

Diana What do we drink to?

Ben That's up to you, Diana. You must decide. But whatever we do, go or stay, you have my word, I'll back you all the way.

They sit on the sofa

Diana This parish, Wychcombe, I know it's just what you've always wanted.

Ben It isn't about a comfy billet, is it though? I'm a priest, that's what I do. There are other parishes, other appointments. Apart from my work, there's us; that's the most important thing.

Diana (*holding up her glass*) To us, then.

Ben I'll drink to that.

They drink a toast. Ben puts his arm round Diana and her head falls on his shoulder

Diana (*yawning*) I'm so tired. I'll think about it in the morning. (*She falls asleep; her glass droops*)

Ben That's right. Sleep on it. God bless you, darling. (*He removes the glass from her hand*)

CURTAIN

FURNITURE AND PROPERTY LIST

ACT I
Scene 1

On stage: Coal scuttle and shovel by fireplace
Fireguard
Sofa. *Behind it*: table with decanter of sherry, unopened bottle of sherry, several glasses
Armchairs
Desk. *On it*: lamp, papers (including sermon and list of builders' snags), pens, notepad, telephone. *In drawer*: set of architect's plans
Chair. *On it*: curtain
Sewing kit
Coffee table
Wastepaper basket
On carpet by french windows: piece of mud
Curtains closed

Off stage: Newspaper (**Diana**)
Garden rake (**Jessy**)
Mug of tea (**Diana**)
Placard with a crude swastika on it (**Jessy**)
Several heads of garlic (**Jessy**)

Personal: **Diana**: sheet of foil-wrapped pills
Ben: fifty pence piece

Scene 2

Strike: Curtain

Off stage: Plate of snacks (**Diana**)
Small knife (**Diana**)

Personal: **Meg**: bag containing small flat plaque wrapped in gift paper
Jessy: key

Scene 3

Set: Garden earth and leaf on carpet
                 Curtain draped over back of armchair

Off stage: Dead rat (**Jessy Impostor/Stage Management**)
                 Two mugs of tea (**Diana**)
                 Umbrella (**Diana**)

Personal: **Jessy**: gardening knife
                 Ben: blood sac

ACT II

Scene 1

Off stage: Cardboard box tied up with string (**Tim**)
                 Book (**Emmeline**)
                 Bunch of flowers (**Peter**)
                 Crude-looking doll (**Tim**)

Personal: **Ben**: handkerchief

Scene 2

Off stage: Suitcase (**Meg**)
                 Empty milk bottle (**Meg**)
                 Torch (**Peter**)
                 Two tea towels (**Peter**)

LIGHTING PLOT

Practical fittings required: desk lamp, coal fire effect
One interior with exterior backing to windows. The same throughout

ACT I, Scene 1

To open: Dim early morning lighting on interior and exterior

Cue 1	**Diana** opens the curtains	(Page 1)
	Bring up interior lights	

ACT I, Scene 2

To open: Mid-day late September lighting on interior and exterior

No cues

ACT I, Scene 3

To open: Gloomy lighting on interior and rain effect on exterior

Cue 2	**Ben** switches on room lights	(Page 28)
	Snap on general interior lighting	

ACT II, Scene 1

To open: Mid-morning late September light on interior and exterior

No cues

ACT II, Scene 2

To open: Evening late September light on interior; darkness on exterior. Fire effect in fireplace

Cue 3	**Meg** sticks note in milk bottle	(Page 48)
	Cut interior lights except fire glow	
Cue 4	**Meg** reaches the door	(Page 48)
	Flicker interior lights then return to opening state	

Cue 5	**Meg** switches off the lights *Cut interior lights except fire glow*	(Page 48)
Cue 6	**Meg** settles on the sofa *Black-out*	(Page 48)
Cue 7	When ready *Bring up firelight slowly*	(Page 48)
Cue 8	**Meg** switches on the lights *Bring up interior lights*	(Page 48)
Cue 9	**Peter** switches on the desk lamp *Snap on desk lamp*	(Page 48)
Cue 10	**Meg** turns off the main light *Cut interior lights except fire glow and desk lamp*	(Page 49)
Cue 11	**Peter** turns off the desk lamp *Snap off desk lamp*	(Page 54)
Cue 12	**Peter** turns on the desk lamp *Snap on desk lamp*	(Page 54)
Cue 13	**Ben** switches on the main light *Bring up interior lights*	(Page 55)

EFFECTS PLOT

ACT I

ACT II

Lightning Source UK Ltd.
Milton Keynes UK
UKOW05f0419280217
295470UK00001B/67/P